D1825156

Who cares?

Childminding in the 1990s

Ann Mooney, Abigail Knight, Peter Moss and Charlie Owen

Published for the Joseph Rowntree Foundation by the
Family Policy Studies Centre
9 Tavistock Place, London WC1H 9SN
Tel: +44 (0)20 7388 5900

ISBN 1 901455 62 9

April 2001

© FPSC/JRF 2001

British Library Catalogue-in-Publication Data
A catalogue record for this book is available from the British
Library.

The **Family Policy Studies Centre** is an independent body which
analyses family trends and the impact of policy. It is a centre of
research and information. The Centre's Governing Council
represents a wide spectrum of political opinion, as well as
professional, academic, faith, local authority and other interests.
The facts presented and views expressed in this report are those of
the author and not necessarily those of the Centre.

The **Joseph Rowntree Foundation** has supported this project as
part of its programme of research and innovative development
projects, which it hopes will be of value to policy-makers,
practitioners and service users. The facts presented and views
expressed in this report, however, are those of the authors and not
necessarily those of the Foundation.

Design and print by Intertype

Photographs by Judy Harrison (front),
Lisa Woollett, Paula Glassman (back) / Format

Contents

1   **Introduction** *7*

2   **Statistical background** *15*

3   **Childminding as an occupation** *20*

4   **How childminders see their work** *39*

5   **Childminders and parents** *48*

6   **Declining numbers of childminders** *59*

7   **Conclusions and issues** *66*

References *70*

Tables and figures

Table 3.1   Characteristics of survey and case study childminders   *20*

Table 3.2   Childminders' ratings on the importance of aspects of their work   *26*

Table 3.3   Non-qualification training undertaken in the last three years   *32*

Table 3.4   Reasons for not attending training courses   *33*

Table 4.1   Childminders' ratings of the importance of goals in their work   *39*

Table 4.2   What parents want from their childminder   *41*

Table 4.3   What childminders find most satisfying about childminding   *44*

Table 4.4   What childminders find most dissatisfying about childminding   *45*

Table 5.1   Views on whether mothers should work, by age of child   *48*

Table 5.2   What parents look for when choosing a childminder   *51*

Figure 2.1   Registered childminders   *15*

Figure 2.2   Children looked after as a percentage of all children   *16*

Figure 2.3   Children looked after by childminders   *17*

Figure 2.4   Childcare arrangements as a percentage of all children   *18*

Figure 3.1   Number of years childminding   *21*

Figure 3.2   Educational qualifications for childminders and nursery nurses   *22*

Figure 3.3   Main reason for becoming a childminder   *23*

Figure 3.4   Hours spent training in preparation for childminding   *25*

Figure 3.5   Who childminders turn to for help   *34*

Figure 3.6   Current work preferences   *36*

Figure 4.1   Satisfaction with working as a childminder   *43*

Figure 6.1   Main reason to stop childminding   *63*

Box 1.1   Regulation of childminders   *8*

Box 1.2   Topics covered by the survey and case studies   *12*

Box 1.3   Characteristics of the two authorities from which case studies drawn   *13*

About the authors

Ann Mooney, Abigail Knight, Peter Moss and Charlie Owen are researchers at the Thomas Coram Research Unit, Institute of Education, University of London

Acknowledgements

We would like to thank the childminders, former childminders and parents who took part in this study. Without their willingness to help this study would not have been possible. We would also like to thank key workers in local authorities, Early Years Development and Childcare Partnerships and the National Childminding Association for their assistance. Christina Moore was involved in the latter stages of the study and we would like to thank her for her contribution. We would like to extend our thanks to the members of our Advisory Group: Shirley Dex, Peter Elfer, Rebecca Goldman, Gill Haynes, Sheila Locke, Barbara Nicholls, Sue Owen and Norma Raynes, who provided valuable support and advice. Finally, we would like to thank the Joseph Rowntree Foundation, who commissioned this research, and particularly Barbara Ballard, who supported us throughout the course of the study.

1 | Introduction

Childminding at the end of the 1980s

Childminding is an important part of the social and economic fabric. It provides an important service to many families and employers and to the wider community. It is also a major source of employment. It is this aspect on which the report focuses: childminding as an occupation, at the end of the twentieth century.

In the late 1980s, the Thomas Coram Research Unit (TCRU) conducted a review of the research done to date in the UK on childminding (Moss, 1987). It drew a number of conclusions about childminders and childminding as an occupation at that time:

- childminding was mainly undertaken by women when their own children were young;
- many women took up the work because it enabled them to combine paid work with caring for their own children. Other factors likely to influence women to go into childminding included the lack of alternative employment and childcare, personal beliefs about childcare and employment, and the intrinsic appeal of the work;
- pay was very low, which was likely to mean that childminding had more appeal to women who had fewer alternative employment opportunities;
- childminders generally had low levels of education, with around three-quarters having left school at 16 or younger, and more than half having no educational qualifications;
- turnover was high, with many childminders moving on as their own children got older or when better employment became available;
- some researchers had proposed two broad groups of childminders: 'short-termers' who

remained childminders for a few years, and 'career minders' who did the job for a long time;
- workload (the number of children cared for and the hours of care provided) varied considerably, including between areas, with highest workloads in the London area. Many childminders had vacancies, again especially outside London, and a substantial proportion of children were at childminders on a part-time basis;
- many childminders provided for children under and over five;
- an estimated 15%–25% of all minded children under five were with unregistered childminders.

The findings of this review provide a baseline against which to compare the situation recounted in this report.

The changing environment for childminding

Since then much has changed in the environment within which childminders work. The policy context has altered substantially. First, there was the Children Act 1989, implemented in 1991. This legislation introduced a modernised system of regulation, covering provision for children up to the age of eight years and intended to 'ensure services meet acceptable standards and ensure an agreed framework for the provision of services' (DH, 1991: para. 4.9). Although subject to regulation beforehand, childminders had to re-register. They became subject to more systematic and thorough inspection (see Box 1.1), with new requirements placed on them – which did not, however, include a requirement for training.

Box 1.1: Regulation of childminders

Although childminders are self-employed, they must be registered with their local authority. The regulations governing the registration of childminders are set out in the Children Act 1989.

Local authorities must register anyone who is looking after children:

- under the age of eight
- for more than two hours a day
- for reward.

People wishing to become childminders must make an application to their local authority and pay a registration fee currently (2000) set at £12.50.

Following receipt of an application, the local authority assesses the suitability of the *person* to provide childcare and the suitability of the *premises* to be used for childminding. Health, safety and police checks are carried out on all household members over the age of 16. During the registration assessment, prospective childminders are visited at home and may be asked to attend pre-registration training and/or briefing sessions.

The conditions of registration include limits on the numbers and ages of children who may be looked after. Under current recommendations childminders can care for no more than three children under the age of five, including their own children. Following registration, childminders are inspected annually by their local authority.

The Children Act also provided new opportunities for childminders. It gave local authorities the power to provide support to childminders and other day care providers, including training, advice and counselling. It also recognised and encouraged a trend noted in the 1987 TCRU review, namely the increasing use of childminders by local authorities, mainly for children 'at risk'. The Children Act placed a duty on local authorities to provide services for children deemed to be 'in need' according to certain broad criteria, and defined childminding as one of the support services that local authorities might use to meet this obligation.

A further change in the regulatory regime is imminent. From September 2001, responsibility for regulation of childminders will be transferred from the social services departments of local authorities to a national agency, the Early Years Directorate of the Office for Standards in Education (OFSTED),

which is also assuming responsibility for other private childcare provision, including day nurseries. At the same time, a new set of national standards for OFSTED to apply is being prepared. Childminding will, therefore, be brought within a framework of regulation that is both national and part of the education system. This is one consequence of the transfer of responsibility in 1997, from the Department of Health to the Department for Education and Employment (DfEE), for what the Children Act called 'day care services'.

Policy developments in the 1990s have gone well beyond changes in the regulation of the private childcare market, an established role for public policy. For many years government had asserted that it was the private responsibility of working parents to make childcare arrangements, either informally (for example, through the use of relatives) or through buying services in a private market, which included childminders; any support for parents was expected to come from employers. Now, first with the childcare disregard introduced by the Conservative Government in 1994, then with the Childcare Tax Credit introduced by the Labour Government in 1999, public policy has extended to subsidising the childcare costs of lower-income working parents. Various measures have also been introduced to stimulate the growth of childcare places under the local aegis of Early Years Development and Childcare Partnerships (EYDCPs).

These developments have taken place within the context of the National Childcare Strategy, whose overall aim is 'to ensure good quality, affordable childcare for children aged 0 to 14 in every neighbourhood, including both formal childcare and support for informal arrangements' (DfEE, 1998:6). Most recently, in 2000, start-up grants for new childminders have been introduced as part of the Strategy, in an attempt to increase recruitment. Another development in policy has been the extension of part-time educational provision to all three- and four-year-olds. Childminders have been given the opportunity to contribute to this provision, as part of an approved childminders' network.

During the latter part of the 1990s, therefore, a direct public policy interest in childcare – for economic and social reasons – has been firmly established, and childminding is clearly recognised as part of that interest.

Demand and supply

These policy changes have been paralleled by changes in *demand for, and supply of, childcare*. Demand has been affected by a rapid growth in employment amongst women with children under five, which began in the second half of the 1980s. Between 1988 and 1998, the employment rate for this group of women rose from 36 per cent to 50 per cent, with full-time employment accounting for nearly half of this increase (Thair and Risden, 1999: Table C). The strongest growth in employment has been among women with higher qualifications and women who are married with employed partners (Brannen *et al.*, 1997; Holtermann *et al.*, 1999).

At the same time, the supply of other forms of childcare has grown, leading potentially to more competition in a childcare system that operates on market principles. In particular, there has been a large increase in the provision of private day nurseries; as we shall show in Chapter Two, nurseries and childminders are providing (and competing) for similar socio-economic groups of parents. Between 1989 and 2000, the number of private day nurseries more than quadrupled, from 1,700 to 7,100, while the number of registered places in these nurseries grew more than five-fold, from 45,000 to 245,100 (DfEE 1999a, 2000). Put another way, in 1989 there were 4.1 registered places with childminders for every one private day nursery place; in 2000, the proportion was just 1.3:1. There has also been a large increase in centre-based school-aged childcare, from fewer than 200 centres in 1990 to almost 6,000 in 2000 (Kids Clubs Network, 2000) – and it is important to remember that around 40 per cent of children who are cared for by childminders are of school age (EO/IDeA, 1999).

National Childminding Association

Last but not least, there is the evolving role of the National Childminding Association (NCMA). NCMA was established in 1977. Its membership grew rapidly in the 1980s from 5,000 to 30,000, about half of all registered childminders. Since then, the NCMA has become an even more important player on the increasingly high-profile childcare scene. It has organised childminders as an occupational group, represented their interests and provided services and other support, organising and stimulating innovative methods and practices, particularly training.

Recent research on childminding as an occupation

Since the 1980s childminding in Britain has changed considerably. It has become more recognised, more regulated, more organised and, potentially, more in demand. At the same time it has faced more competition from other types of formal childcare. How has research kept pace with these changes?

There have been a number of new research studies bearing on childminding as an occupation. The development and use of childminding for children 'in need' has been the subject of research (Dillon and Statham, 1998a, 1998b; Statham et al., 2000; Moss et al., 2000) and work has been undertaken on the new regulatory regime introduced by the Children Act and the response of childminders (Bull et al., 1994; Candappa et al., 1996; Moss et al., 1995).

The workforce, in particular their past training and future training needs, was the subject of a national survey conducted in 1999 by the Employers' Organisation/ Improvement and Development Agency (EO/ IdeA), previously known as the Local Government Management Board (EO/IDeA, 1999). A large national sample, 30 per cent of all registered childminders, was taken, although the low response rate (26 per cent) means the results must be treated with

caution. Two findings stand out: childminders are more likely to have a background of paid or voluntary childcare *experience* (eg. in playgroups) than relevant *qualifications*; and a high annual turnover, estimated to be at least 18 per cent (the figure for day nursery staff, from a parallel survey, was also high at 16 per cent). We will compare results from this national sample, and our own, later in this report.

More intensive work has been undertaken with smaller and local samples which cannot claim to be representative nationally. Working at the beginning of the 1990s, Ferri (1992) studied 30 childminders. One of her conclusions raises issues we will return to:

'It may be hypothesised that not only will childminders be in shrinking supply, but that the typical profile of such providers may alter. An earlier return to the labour market may mean that childminding, if undertaken at all, is pursued for shorter periods, and more predominantly by women whose own children are very young' (Ferri, 1992:198).

Working later in the decade, Gelder (1998) focused on the social and economic conditions of childminders. She combined a postal survey of 475 childminders in the north east of England, (a 43 per cent response rate), and in-depth interviews with ten childminders. Her research investigated the relationship between childminding as an occupation and home-based work, gender and family life:

'The work of a childminder is characterised by a constant tension between the tasks arising out of her private role as mother and housewife and her public role as childminder ... [T]hey take their role as mother and housewife very seriously; on the other hand they like to be their own boss and see themselves as a childcare professional' (Gelder, 1998:10).

Ferri also focused attention on the complex, ambivalent and potentially fraught relationship between motherhood and childminding, both home-based activities:

'The greatest influence over a childminder's approach to day-care provision is thus the shape and substance of her own family life … [with an] equation of the role of childminder with that of parent … [Consequently] childminders are strongly resistant to the notion that, as mothers, they have anything to learn about how to provide for children … It is essential in our view that those responsible for childminding and childminder training grasp the nettle of clarifying the boundaries between what childminders do as parents and what they should do as caregivers'
(Ferri, 1992:190, 192).

Finally, there has been an increasing amount of cross-national work, which illustrates the variability of childminding across countries (Karlsson, 1995). (Outside the UK childminding is usually known as family day care.) In particular, this cross-national work has described different ways of organising childminding, ranging from childminders employed as members of organised schemes, managed by local authorities or private organisations (eg. in the Nordic countries), to self-employed childminders operating independently in a private market (as in the UK and the USA). Once again, this raises questions about the work itself, not only the conditions of employment but also the status of childminding:

'In many countries there is a discussion about whether a family day-carer should see herself as a professional or not … The argument against is that anyone can become a family day carer: there are no special demands for training or standards of quality involved. Others argue that a professional family day carer might lose her 'genuine motherly feeling' and some of her flexibility. The argument for professionalisation is the need for recognition of the importance of the work done …, the necessity of setting up some minimum standards and the family day carers' wish to receive social rights in the labour market' (Karlsson, 1995:61).

Introducing the study and the report

Childminding as an occupation

This report presents the main findings from a study undertaken at TCRU between January 1999 and November 2000. The study was part of the Joseph Rowntree Foundation (JRF) Work and Family Life Programme. Its purpose was to investigate registered childminders (see Box 1.1) as a distinct occupational group within the total childcare workforce. It has been complemented by government-funded research at TCRU on nursery workers (Cameron, Owen and Moss, forthcoming). More specifically, the initial aims of the study were to examine:

- the place of childminding within the overall provision of childcare for children with employed parents;
- the education and employment histories of childminders, including when and why people become childminders, their future employment intentions and when and why they leave the work;

- the working conditions of childminders, including pay, training and support; and
- childminders' views about their work and their job satisfaction.

This part of the study involved:

- *secondary analysis* of the Family Resource Survey, a large-scale annual survey undertaken for Government since 1993, which asks questions about childcare use;
- *a postal survey* of a representative national sample of childminders. A sample of 1,050 childminders was randomly selected from lists held by eight local authorities, also randomly selected to give a representative spread, both geographically and by type of authority. Childminders were asked to complete a questionnaire designed to elicit information about their training and employment histories, working conditions and views about, and commitment, to their work. Issues considered included: when and why they became childminders, their hours of work and working conditions and their views about employed parents and the care needs of young children (see Box 1.2 for further information). Most questions invited

closed responses although respondents had the opportunity to add comments at the end of the questionnaire. A good response rate was achieved (62 per cent), although to our surprise nearly a quarter of the responding childminders (23 per cent) said they were not currently minding, despite being on their local authority's list – they had either stopped altogether or were taking a break from work. This left us with 497 childminders who both responded and were currently working as childminders;

- *case studies* of 30 childminders, 15 each from two different areas (a city area and a suburban area, both in the south east, details of which are provided in Box 1.3), divided further into three groups: new childminders, registered in the last year; established childminders; and childminders who had recently stopped childminding. The childminders in each group were randomly selected. In-depth interviews lasting one to two hours were conducted with each childminder. Topics covered in the interview are listed in Box 1.2.

The interviews were taped, transcribed and

Box 1.2: Topics covered by the survey and case studies

Topics	Survey	Cases
Demographic information	Yes	Yes
Reasons for becoming a childminder	Yes	Yes
Working conditions	Yes	Yes
Views about childcare	Yes	Yes
Previous employment	Yes	Yes
Satisfaction with childminding work	Yes	Yes
Commitment to childminding work	Yes	Yes
Attitude towards regulation	No	Yes
Experience of homeworking	No	Yes
Relationship with parents and children	No	Yes

Box 1.3: Characteristics of the two authorities from which case studies drawn

Authority A: City area

A diverse multi-cultural authority with a population of around 216,000. It is one of the most deprived authorities in England. There are low levels of educational qualifications among the adult population and a high incidence of lone-parent families and families on Housing Benefit. Forty one per cent of primary school pupils are eligible for free school meals. The unemployment rate is around 10 per cent, although there are areas where the rate is much higher. Local employment opportunities are limited, particularly for those who are skilled. The local authority and health trust are the largest local employers.

321 childminders (228 are active)

3 LEA combined nursery centres

3 LEA under-fives centres

57 LEA nursery classes

29 nurseries (private/voluntary sector)

27 pre-school groups

28 after-school clubs

Much of the provision for three- and four-year-olds is in the maintained sector and childminders are the main providers for the under threes. There has been a decline in the number of registered childminders, which is thought to reflect the updating of the register.

The highest percentage of childminders are from the African–Caribbean community. Registration and inspection is separate from development and support, which is undertaken by the Quality Assurance Team. Each childminder receives a training prospectus and there were 105 childminder enrolments on a range of courses in 1999-2000. A training course 'Preparation for Becoming a Childminder' is offered and comprises of six half-day sessions. It is expected that those wishing to register will attend.

Authority B: Suburban area

A relatively prosperous authority with a population of over a million and with both urban and rural areas. However, there are significant pockets of social and economic deprivation. Around 10 per cent of primary school pupils are eligible for free school meals. Unemployment is low at 2 per cent. There have been increases in employment in the banking section and decreases in manufacturing. Distribution and public administration are the two main sources of employment.

3,097 childminders (all active)

235 LEA nursery classes

17 LEA nursery schools

89 nurseries (private/voluntary sector)

363 pre-school groups

66 after-school clubs

Fewer than 2 per cent of childminders are from minority ethnic backgrounds. Registration and inspection is combined with support and development work. The authority is divided into four areas and each has a number of drop-in centres.

Prospective childminders are invited to a pre-registration information session before making an application. Although pre-registration training is not a requirement of registration, all childminders are encouraged to attend two four-week training modules in their first year. Each module totals eight hours of training. The Childcare Audit for 1999 records that only 42 per cent of childminders report any relevant training.

analysed using NUD*IST, the computer assisted qualitative data analysis software. In addition, shorter telephone interviews were conducted with 21 parents of children cared for by the new and established childminders. While offering an important perspective on childminding, these parents constituted a small sample which cannot be viewed as representative.

Decrease in childminder numbers

Towards the end of the initial study, it became apparent that the number of registered childminders was falling quite rapidly (see Chapter Two). The JRF extended the project to enable further work to understand better what was happening and why.

The extension adopted a number of approaches to examine the apparent decrease in childminder numbers. An analysis was conducted, at local authority level, of official government statistics between 1996 and 1999, to see if changes in childminder numbers were systematically related to changes in other types of childcare and early education provision. One aim was to examine if there was a statistical relationship between falling childminder numbers and rising day-nursery places which, if found, might suggest that some childminders were being squeezed out by the expansion of other forms of childcare. Next, visits were made to ten local authorities which, according to official statistics, showed high rates of decrease in childminder numbers. Interviews were conducted with key workers to explore their views on the reasons for falling numbers. This

work was complemented by a postal survey of 140 EYDCPs (the ten local authorities to be visited were excluded), to ask if they had conducted any investigations related to falling childminder numbers. Of the 97 that responded (67 per cent response rate), 39 per cent had undertaken, or were undertaking, studies in this area, usually exit questionnaires. Finally, interviews were conducted with national and regional staff of the NCMA, who also provided some valuable information from their membership records.

The study, and this report, is limited to childminding in England. Although childminding in Scotland, Wales and Northern Ireland may share many features with England, we cannot lay claim to speak about these other parts of Britain. So, when we say 'national', we refer only to England.

In the next chapter we look at childminding statistically, based on our analysis of the FRS and official statistics: how many childminders are there and what contribution do they make to childcare overall? Using our own survey case-study data, Chapters Three to Five look in detail at childminding as an occupation, how childminders see their work and the relationship between childminders and parents. Chapter Six examines the phenomenon of the apparently falling number of childminders: is there really a drop in numbers and, if so, what might be the reasons? Finally, in Chapter Seven, we summarise the main conclusions from the research and consider some of the issues they raise, including the future of childminding.

2 | Statistical background

How many childminders?

Every year, local authorities make returns to government (prior to 1998 to the Department of Health, since then to the Department for Education and Employment) of the number of registered 'day care' providers on their books. Between 1989 and 2000 the national figures for registered childminders have fluctuated (DfEE, 2000). From 1989 to 1992 the number increased, from 83,900 to 109,200; it then wobbled up and down until 1996, before beginning a consistent downward trend, falling from 102,600 to 75,600 in 2000 (see Figure 2.1). We consider the possible reasons for this fall in Chapter Six.

These national returns also include the number of places available for children at childminders. In 1989 there were 2.2 places per registered childminder; this figure rose to 4.2 in 2000. The number of children a childminder is registered for may be more than they actually care for or are willing to care for. The childminders in our 1999 postal survey reported being registered for 4.8 children, on average. However, they were actually caring for 3.5 children (very similar to the 3.7 recorded in the 1999 EO/IDeA study), and half said they had vacancies. Gelder (1998) reports even higher vacancy levels, with childminders averaging only two children

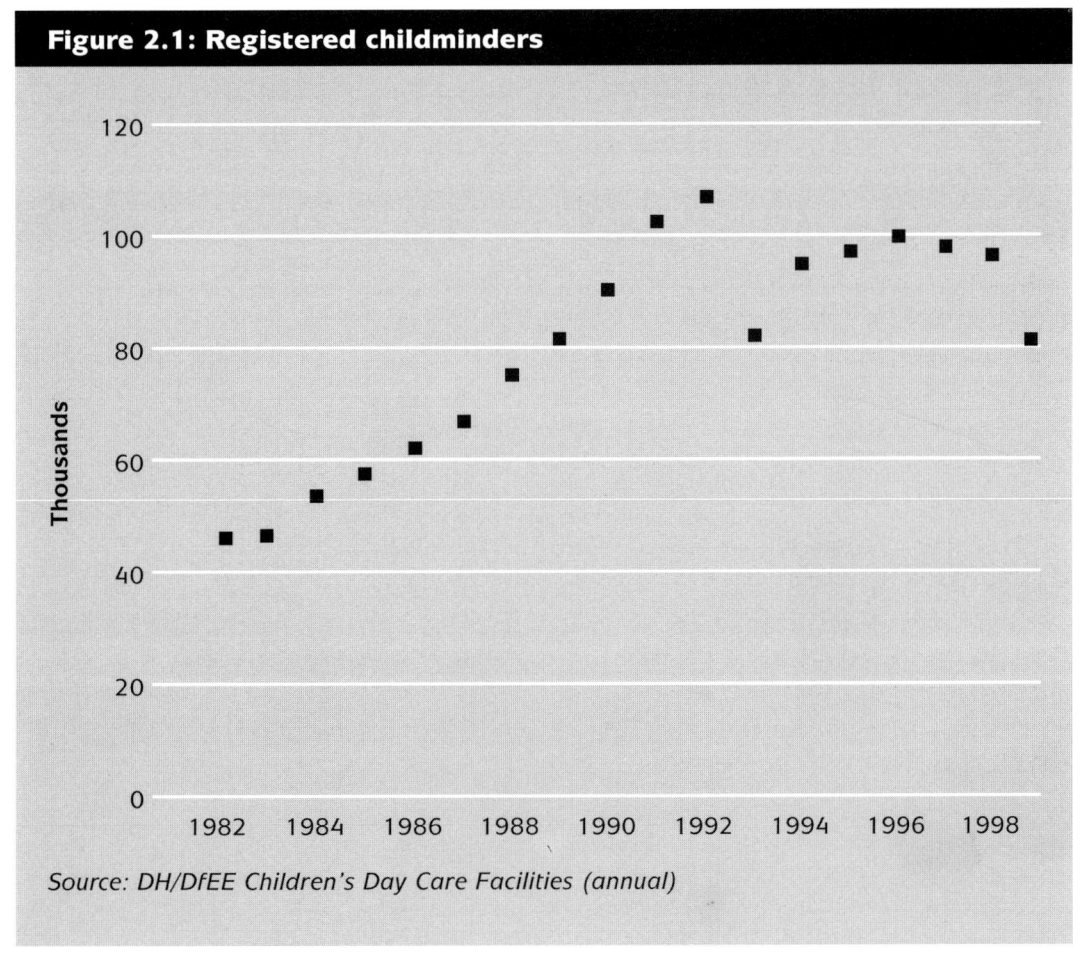

Figure 2.1: Registered childminders

Source: DH/DfEE Children's Day Care Facilities (annual)

despite being registered to take up to six children; this may, however, reflect the relatively poor employment situation in the north east of England where Gelder's study was conducted. A national survey of all types of childcare providers found that two-thirds of childminders had had vacancies in the preceding year, fewer than other types of provider, where nearly four out of five had had vacancies (Callender, 2000). Furthermore, as already noted, a quarter of our respondents actually said they had stopped minding, permanently or temporarily, even though their names had been obtained from their local authority's list of active childminders. All this points to the places actually in use at registered childminders being substantially less than those recorded as available.

Overall, these national statistics raise as many questions as they answer. Their meaning is difficult to 'read'. To what extent do they reflect real changes, or changes in legislative definitions or, indeed, changes in how the statistics themselves are produced? We will return to this issue in Chapter Six when we explore in more detail whether the number of childminders is really decreasing.

The place of childminding in the childcare picture

Our analysis of the FRS for 1993–1996 revealed a familiar picture of childcare arrangements while parents are working (Figure 2.2). Many parents manage work and childcare without using *non-parental* care, usually by mothers doing part-time work when their partners are not at work and can therefore take over childcare at home. But for those children under five years of age receiving some form of *non-parental care* while their

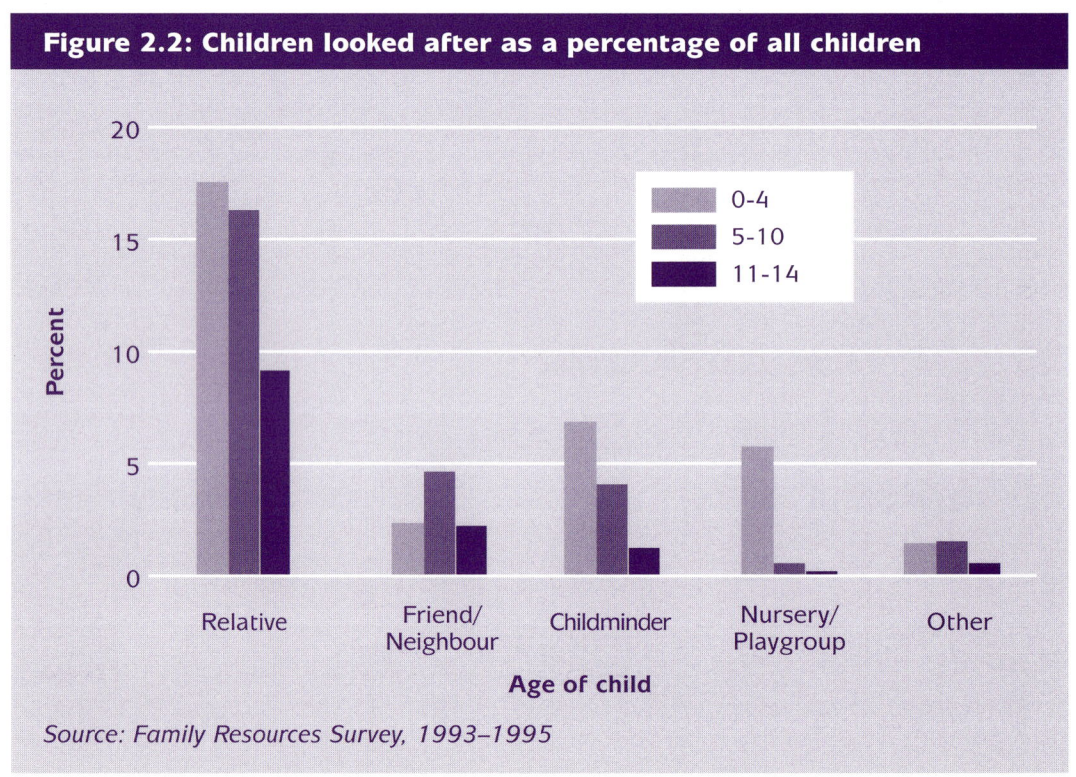

Figure 2.2: Children looked after as a percentage of all children

Source: Family Resources Survey, 1993–1995

parents were at work, by far the most common arrangement (58 per cent) was care by relatives, with a further 8 per cent cared for by friends and neighbours. Next, some way behind, but leading the formal providers, came childminders: they accounted for nearly a quarter of under-fives receiving non-parental care (22 per cent), or nearly 6 per cent of all under-fives. 'Nurseries and playgroups' (the FRS does not distinguish between these forms of provision) provided for 19 per cent of children getting non-parental care or 5 per cent of all under-fives. Finally, a long way behind came an 'other' group, which includes nannies and au pairs, accounting for just 5 per cent of childcare – 1 per cent of all under-fives. The same pattern was true for children aged five to ten years.

We say 'familiar picture', because all surveys of arrangements made by working parents for the non-parental care of their children *while they (the parents) are at work* show the same findings. Parents sharing care and informal care mainly by relatives (and then mainly by grandmothers) are far ahead of the field, with childminders being the main providers of formal childcare (Bridgewood and Savage, 1993; Daniel, 1980; Martin and Roberts, 1984; McRae and Daniel, 1991; Marsh and McKay, 1993).

Childcare arrangements are not, however, uniform across the population. There is consistent evidence that they vary substantially between socio-economic groups. The FRS analysis, for instance, shows that the great majority of mothers and fathers using

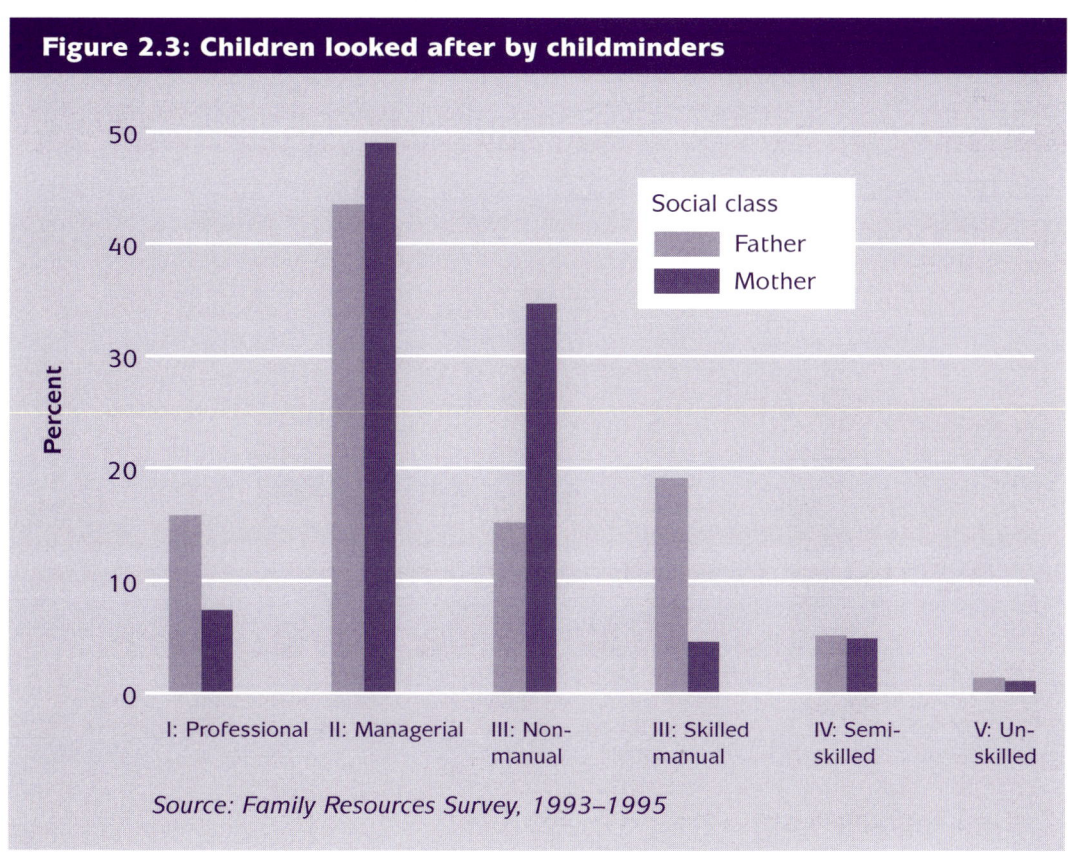

Figure 2.3: Children looked after by childminders

Source: *Family Resources Survey, 1993–1995*

childminders worked full-time and that most (56 per cent of mothers, 59 per cent of fathers) were in professional and managerial jobs (Figure 2.3). The two are related, with mothers in higher status jobs (and with higher educational qualifications) being more likely to be in paid work overall and, if working, being more likely to work full time (Holtermann *et al.*, 1999). The profile of childminder users, according to our FRS analysis, was very similar to the day nursery/playgroup users (Figure 2.4). It differed, however, from the profile of parents using relatives and friends, who were much less likely to work in managerial or professional jobs (30 per cent of mothers, 35 per cent of fathers), while the mothers were more likely to work part time (18 per cent using relatives or friends, 6 per cent using childminders).

These socio-economic differences are observed in other studies. A government

survey of 'day care services' for children under five, conducted in 1991, reported that regular care by relatives:

'increased with decreasing social class. For example, 18 per cent of children in households classified as professional were regularly cared for by grandparents compared with 44 per cent of children in households headed by an unskilled manual worker. The proportion of children of working mothers looked after by a childminder in social class I, 18 per cent, was twice that of social class V. Of course these differences may reflect different attitudes between different classes but they may also reflect income differences. Practically all nannies or mothers' helps looked after children of professionals, employers and managers' (Meltzer, 1994: 19).

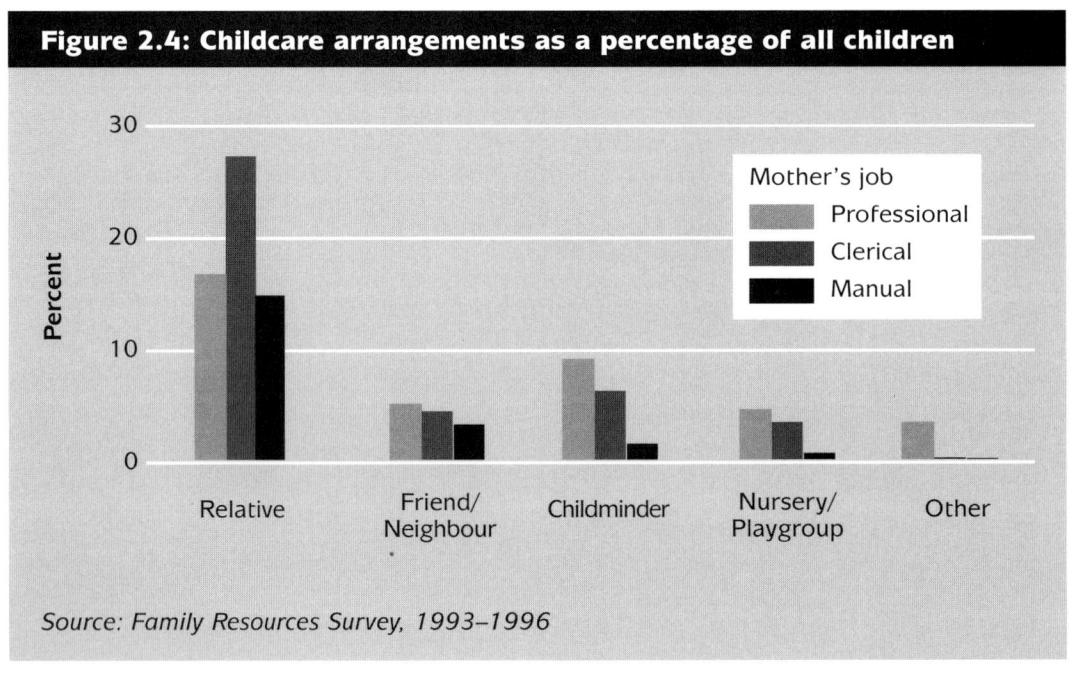

Figure 2.4: Childcare arrangements as a percentage of all children

Source: Family Resources Survey, 1993–1996

The 1999 government-funded survey of 'parents' demand for childcare', conducted in 1999, also found socio-economic differences. A child in social class I or II was '51 per cent more likely to receive formal childcare, when compared with a child living in social class III manual ... [While] the odds of a child living in a family in the highest income group receiving formal childcare was 2.6 times higher than a child living in a household with an income below £10,400' (LaValle et al., 2000:43). Childminders were the most common type of formal childcare used by couples where both worked full time and by lone parents who worked full time, and their use increased with household income, from 3 per cent for the lowest income group to 17 per cent for the highest.

Summary

Childminding continues to play an important part in the provision of childcare for working parents, maintaining its position as the most common type of formal provision. Surveys of childcare use show consistent socio-economic differences, with parents in lower socio-economic groups more likely to use informal arrangements. Most of the parents who use childminders for the care of their children work full time and in higher status (and better paid) jobs.

3 | Childminding as an occupation

As discussed in Chapter One, there are a few British research studies which have looked at different aspects of working as a childminder (eg. Ferri, 1992; Gelder 1998; EO/IDeA, 1999). Other studies conducted in the US, Canada and Australia (eg. Atkinson, 1991; Nelson, 1989; Pence and Goelman, 1991; Saggers et al., 1994) add to this body of knowledge, although the circumstances of childminding in these other countries may be different. The reasons for working as a childminder, as reported in British, North American and Australian studies, are a desire to be at home, combined with a love of children and not wishing to use non-parental childcare for their own children (Mayall and Petrie 1983; Nelson, 1989; Saggers, 1994). Several North American studies have found a significant relationship between provider training and quality of care (eg. Fischer and Eheart, 1991; Fosburg, 1981; Howes, 1983; Kontos et al., 1995; Pence and Goelman,

1991). Pence and Goleman, for example, found that the quality of care provided by Canadian childminders was higher among those who had undertaken specific formal training, saw childminding as a profession and who wanted to continue working as a childminder for some considerable time. This chapter looks first at the characteristics of the survey and case study childminders, before turning to look at the motivation for becoming a childminder, training and preparation for childminding, the conditions of work and childminding as work.

Becoming a childminder

Childminder characteristics
Demographics:
Table 3.1 summarises the demographic data.
Survey: Only two of the 497 childminders in the survey were men. Over three-quarters of the sample were aged between 25 and 44,

Table 3.1 Characteristics of survey and case study childminders

	Survey (n=497) %	Cases (n=30) %
Female	99.6	100
Age 16–24	1.6	-
25–34	28.7	33
35–44	49.5	47
45–54	17.0	20
55–64	3.0	-
65+	0.2	-
Ethnic minorities	3.2	17
Single parent	10.1	23
Own children	98.0	97
A child under five	39.5	40
Three or more children	36.3	47
Own children when started minding	95.0	90
Child under five when started minding	75.0	85

with almost half in the age group 35 to 44. This is a similar result to the EO/IDeA survey. Almost all were white with children of their own. Of those with children, two-fifths had a child under five. Most were living as a couple with partners who were working full-time.

How does this sample of childminders compare with other childcare workers such as nursery nurses? Secondary analysis of the Labour Force Survey 1996–1998 (Cameron *et al.*, forthcoming) shows that nursery nurses are predominately female (99 per cent) as is the childcare workforce as a whole, white (95 per cent), on average younger than childminders (33 per cent aged under 26) and almost a third are single (31 per cent).

On average, survey childminders had been childminding for six years. As can be seen from Figure 3.1, more than half had worked for five years or less, of whom almost a quarter had worked for a year or less. Less than a fifth had been childminding for over ten years. The survey found that childminders do not

necessarily childmind continuously. A quarter had taken a break in their childminding career.

Case study: The case study childminders have a similar demographic profile to those in the survey (Table 3.1), although there were more single-parent households and childminders from minority ethnic groups. This difference may be due to sampling. One of the two authorities for the case studies had a high percentage of childminders from the African–Caribbean community (see Box 1.3). All were women, with an average age of 39 (range 26- to 51-years-old). All but one had children, of whom just under a third were aged under five (range 18 months to 29 years). Among the case study childminders, both the established group of childminders and the ex-childminder group had on average been minding ten years (range 1 to 21 years). Childminders new to childminding had been working for one year or less.

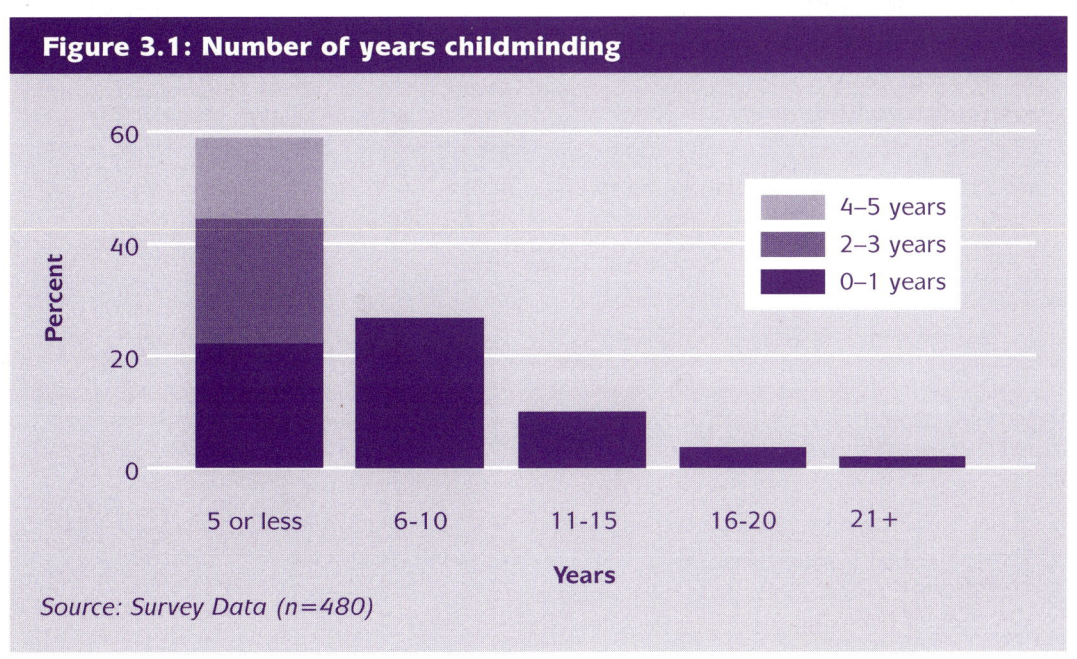

Figure 3.1: Number of years childminding

Source: Survey Data (n=480)

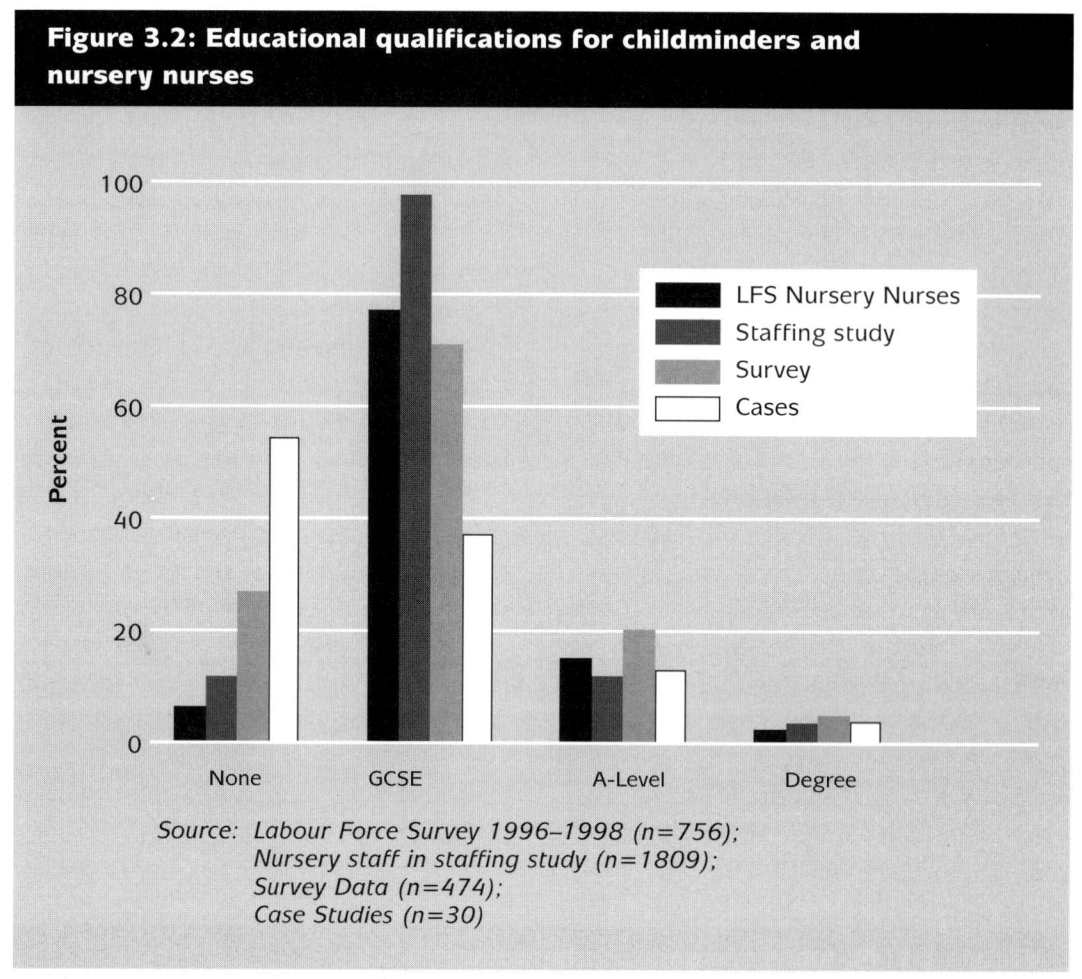

Figure 3.2: Educational qualifications for childminders and nursery nurses

Source: Labour Force Survey 1996–1998 (n=756);
Nursery staff in staffing study (n=1809);
Survey Data (n=474);
Case Studies (n=30)

Educational qualifications

Educational qualifications for survey and case study childminders are compared with nursery nurses in the Labour Force Survey 1996–1998 and the results from a survey of childcare and education staff (excluding officers-in-charge) in 250 nurseries, referred to as the 'staffing study' (Cameron *et al.*, forthcoming). Data on educational qualifications was not collected from the EO/IDeA survey of childminders. As Figure 3.2 shows, childminders in our survey are more likely than nursery nurses to have no formal educational qualifications. The difference may, in part, be due to the fact that childminders are on average older than

nursery nurses and therefore less likely to have left school with a qualification. The number of school leavers leaving school with a qualification has been rising: in 1999, 73 per cent of school leavers held at least one GCSE grade A*–C and 94 per cent held at least one GCSE graded A*–G (DfEE, 1999b). However, Figure 3.2 also shows that within the minority of childminders and nursery nurses with higher educational qualifications (A-level and Degree), childminders in the survey are more likely than nursery nurses to hold a higher qualification.

Childcare qualifications

Less than a quarter (21 per cent) of the childminders in the survey, and 17 per cent of the case-study childminders, had a qualification related to childcare. This compares with about one-third (30 per cent) of childminders in the EO/IDeA survey. These figures are lower than those from surveys of other childcare workers. For example, in the Labour Force Survey 39 per cent of nursery nurses, and 38 per cent of playgroup leaders, had a professional or vocational qualification (Cameron *et al.*, forthcoming).

Previous employment

Most of our survey childminders (92 per cent) had worked in other jobs before becoming childminders. As a group they had worked in a variety of occupations, though predominately semi-skilled and unskilled work in the service sector. Three-quarters had taken a break from employment between their last job and childminding. The average length of this break

was four years, although almost half (46 per cent) were childminding within two years of ending their previous employment. All 30 of the case study childminders had worked in other occupations before childminding, including childcare, shop, clerical and catering work.

Reasons for moving into childminding

Most of the childminders in our survey had at least one pre-school child when they started childminding (Table 3.1). The main reason for entering childminding for the survey childminders was that childminding enabled them to stay at home with their own children or work from home (Figure 3.3).

Case study childminders gave a variety of reasons for becoming a childminder including an enjoyment of being with, and caring for, children (mentioned by one-third), an approach from an acquaintance or friend to look after their child, and providing company for their own children. However, by far the

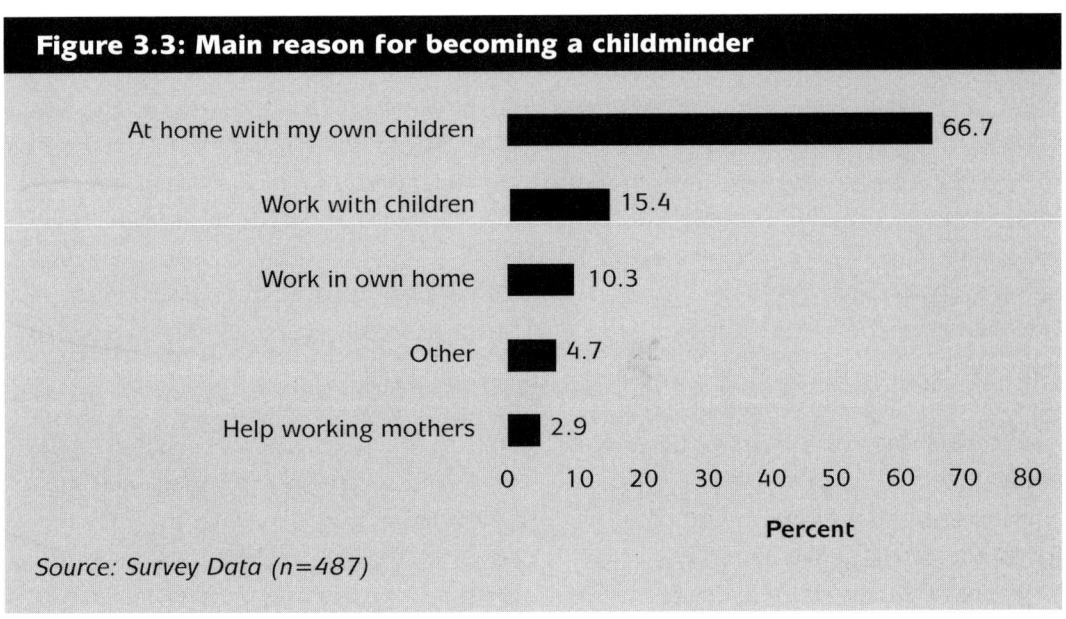

Figure 3.3: Main reason for becoming a childminder

At home with my own children — 66.7
Work with children — 15.4
Work in own home — 10.3
Other — 4.7
Help working mothers — 2.9

Percent

Source: Survey Data (n=487)

most frequently-mentioned reason was that childminding presented the opportunity to be at home with their own children whilst at the same time earning an income. Other surveys also report that the main reason why women workers choose to work at home is to be at home with their children whilst earning an income (Huws, 1994; Felstead and Jewson, 1996). All but two of the case studies depended on the income that childminding brought them. Their contribution to the family budget was important, particularly in the seven lone-parent households where it was the only income, and most would have sought alternative employment if they had not become childminders.

Survey childminders were not asked the reason why they wanted to stay at home with their children, though it may have been due to not wanting to leave their children in the care of someone else as was the case with some case study childminders:

I can't hand my child out to somebody else.

Homeworking was one of the few avenues open to them where they could generate an income and care for their children themselves. However, for many more of the case study childminders, though they may have had a preference not to leave their children, it seemed that their decision to enter childminding was influenced more by the lack of intrinsic rewards and financial benefits that alternative employment offered. As described above, many had few formal educational qualifications. The jobs they were doing before starting a family were unlikely to be highly paid. Having taken childcare costs into consideration, it appears that many would have found alternative employment uneconomical.

Compared with the survey childminders, 31 per cent of whom had worked and used non-maternal childcare, more than half (57 per cent) of the case study childminders had worked outside the home after having children. Their reasons for turning to childminding were threefold. First, the difficulty of finding affordable and suitable childcare:

By the time I'd paid for travel and childcare costs, I was bringing in less than I earn now, working two and a half days from home as a childminder.

Second, having a job that was not fulfilling or which could not be easily fitted in with their childcare:

I'd been doing shop work, which I got fed up with.

Third, the difficulties of balancing home and family life:

I was tired. The housework wasn't getting done … it's time to rush around to get her to school, and get her to my mum's, and get to work. And it was just a nightmare.

Thus, childminding offered:
- the potential to be more rewarding than other employment opportunities available to them;
- being at home with their own children;
- the possibility of better financial rewards than working outside the home and paying for childcare.

In addition, it appeared that registering as a childminder could sometimes be undertaken as a means of ensuring employment in the future. Three of the case studies had registered, but did not immediately start

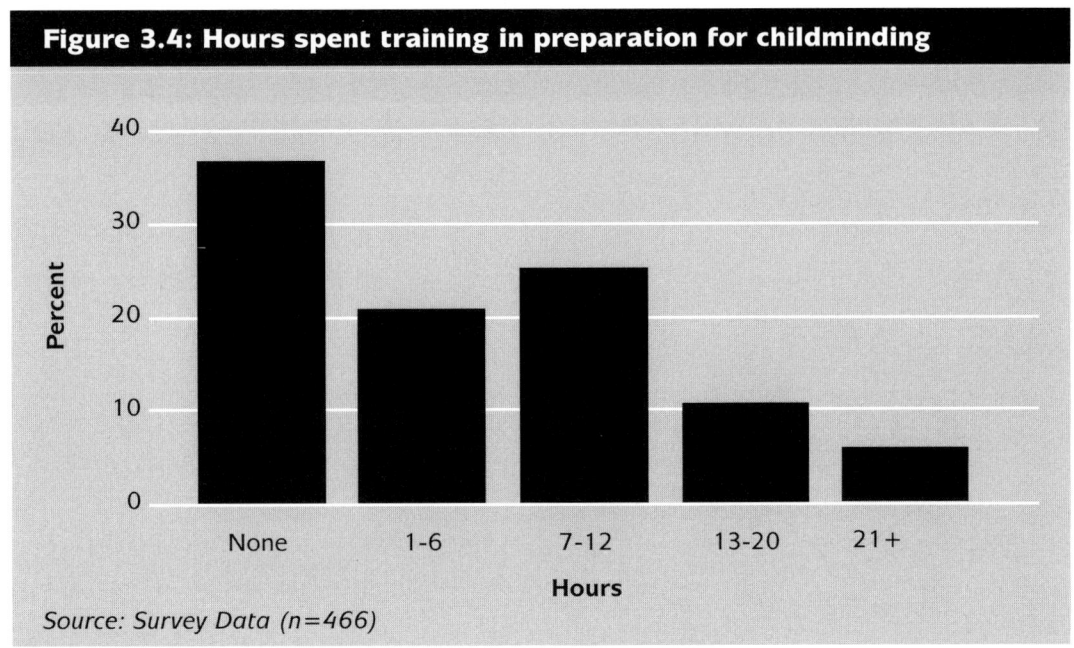

Figure 3.4: Hours spent training in preparation for childminding

Source: Survey Data (n=466)

childminding. One was registered for two years before she became active. It seemed that these women were uncertain about their employment opportunities outside the home and saw childminding as a job to fall back on. This can pose a probem in terms of calculating the number of registered childminders and places if women are reigstered, but not actively childminding.

Training and preparation for childminding

Since the Children Act 1989, many local authorities have introduced training in preparation for becoming a childminder, though the content and duration of such training varies. Figure 3.4 shows the variability in hours that survey childminders had spent in this type of training. Nearly two-thirds (64 per cent) had undertaken training in preparation for childminding. The EO/IDeA survey of childminders reported a similar figure. Those without pre-registration training tended to be

those who had registered more than ten years ago, when training was less common.

Most of the case study childminders said they had received training in preparation for becoming a childminder, although the duration of the training varied. Whereas some childminders were of the opinion that such training did provide a good preparation for childminding, others felt it did not go far enough in preparing them for some of the difficulties they later encountered, such as poor time-keeping and late payment. Some voiced the opinion that there was little that training could offer in these areas and that childminders had to learn through their experiences.

The majority of childminders do see themselves as professional childcare workers (Table 3.2). Yet, less than a quarter considered it very important for childminders to have a childcare qualification and only a third thought it was very important for childminders to attend training courses. This result should

Table 3.2 Childminder's ratings of the importance of aspects of their work				
			Importance	
	N	No %	Somewhat %	Very %
See themselves as professionals	486	5.3	32.1	62.6
Views on child-rearing similar to parents	477	2.7	40.7	56.6
Be parents themselves	484	17.1	31.0	51.9
Opportunities to develop their childcare career	479	8.6	56.6	34.9
Attend childcare training courses	484	13.4	56.0	30.6
Hold a childcare qualification	488	32.2	44.5	23.4

Source: Survey data

been seen in the context of there being no requirement for childminders to have training in childcare. They were divided in their opinion as to the importance of childminders being parents, with just over half thinking it was very important and just under half thinking it was only somewhat or not at all important.

The majority of case study childminders felt that a childcare qualification was less important to them in their work than the experience of being a parent:

Childminding is like – it just needs me being a mother. And I don't really know what sort of qualification you really need.
(new childminder)

An ex-childminder describes the way in which she believes parenthood prepares one for childminding:

I think you only can understand children and have any love for children once you're a mum. Because you can read it in a book and learn how to do it … But the feeling isn't going to be there.

For this group of childminders, training appeared to devalue their parenting skills.

The following comment, from an established childminder with children of her own, illustrates that not all the case study childminders considered it was important for childminders to be parents:

Some people who don't have children might be better childminders than people who do have. They've more time to devote to it to start off … There could be benefits to that.

Those with a childcare qualification were much more likely to say that it is training rather than the experience of parenting which is more valuable.

Case study childminders were asked their views about making attendance at training courses or holding a childcare qualification compulsory for childminders. Some considered it to be a good idea:

I think for everyone in childcare it should be compulsory … I think it's important they should be taught, yes. So, if nothing else, you should give standard care, minimum standard care. (ex-childminder)

Those responding positively thought that people less suited to the profession would be deterred from registering. Furthermore, a qualification would not only give childminders a sense of achievement and recognition, but would help raise the status of childminding. Others were less sure about mandatory training and qualifications, raising concerns about financing courses and finding appropriate childcare for their children.

Getting started as a childminder

Registration and inspection

The regulation of childminders was explored with the case study childminders, but was not covered in the survey. In general, new childminders with less experience of inspections, and not knowing how it may have changed, were less critical than childminders with more years of service. Although negative comments far outweighed the positive, they all focused on the process of regulation. No one suggested that registration and inspection were unnecessary or unimportant.

Positive comments centred on the importance of regulation in ensuring that suitable people are registered and standards of care maintained. Talking about registration, one childminder said:

I actually thought it was very good. As a mother, I wouldn't have liked to have thought that anybody could just go and get registered. That felt right to me. Because I think it would put people off who weren't serious about childcare.

Another believed that the initial assessment was very good, but it didn't go far enough:

They don't try to ask you anything about what your idea of encouraging a child to develop is.

The time taken to register varied considerably between authorities, taking anything from several weeks to a year. Police checks were usually cited by childminders as the reason for the delay. Long delays in registration can be frustrating, not least because most of these women were motivated, in part, by the need for an income and unnecessary delays had financial consequences. Also, some had parents waiting who were becoming quite desperate as the process dragged on. It is possible that lengthy delays in registration may deter many potential childminders as one childminder claimed.

Turning to inspections, several felt that one annual inspection was insufficient for monitoring standards. Asked elsewhere in the interview how childminding could be improved, the most frequent response was that local authority officers should make unannounced visits to childminders:

I think it would possibly stop people from falling into bad habits, and not just making sure their house is fine again the week before they come.

Local authorities differ with respect to the resources available to conduct unannounced visits in addition to the annual inspection (Mooney and Munton, 1999). Many are unable to do them.

Childminders were more critical of the way in which inspections were conducted in Authority A (see Box 1.3, page 13). Inspectors were accused of inflexibility and insensitivity in their demands and a level of repetition or 'red tape' that seemed to some a waste of everyone's time. Sometimes childminders did feel inadequate or personally affronted when criticisms were made of their home. In Authority A which attracted most criticism, childminders with more years of experience recalled earlier times when under-eights officers were more likely to establish a supportive and friendly relationship with childminders. As one childminder observed:

It's completely about monitoring [now]. It's not supposed to be supportive at all.

In this authority three of the ten ex-childminders had stopped childminding because of tighter regulations and frustrations with bureaucracy. It should be noted that this group may have included childminders who had not had their registration renewed, and who therefore might be expected to be more critical of regulation and inspection procedures. However, one established childminder from this authority did say that:

and they [registration and inspection] want so much from you as a childminder … I don't think the money's that great for the hours you do … I wouldn't entertain it if I wasn't a childminder already.

Start-up costs

The expenses that childminders incur when first starting out is an issue that until very recently has received little public attention. Expenses include the cost of registration and insurance, any changes to the home and the purchase of equipment and toys. This financial outlay comes at a time when childminders do not have an income and cannot be sure when they will start earning. As we shall see in the next section, new childminders often had

difficulty in filling their vacancies and waited some months before earning any money. It seemed to some childminders that registration and inspection procedures made no allowances for this situation:

They [registration and inspection] wanted me to get lots of particular toys and some of them were very expensive. I said 'do you have a system where you can borrow them from somewhere first, until you can buy one?' … until you've earned some money, you can't buy fifty pounds, a hundred pounds worth of toys.

That start-up costs can be a real barrier to people becoming childminders has now been recognised by the Government, largely as a result of campaigning by the NCMA, and start-up grants for new childminders have now been introduced.

Finding work

Survey childminders were caring for a total of 1,715 children. Sixty-five per cent of children were aged under five years with two-year-olds being the largest age group, followed by those aged three. Although childminders were registered, on average, for 4.8 children, they were caring for 3.5 children. These results follow the same pattern as those from the EO/IDeA survey.

One half of the childminders said they had vacancies. Vacancies are not necessarily due to problems in finding children, as the case study data highlights. Some childminders chose not to childmind to their capacity, either because it suited their current circumstances or because they felt they could offer a better service and manage·more easily with fewer children. One case study childminder who had two children for 11 hours, three days a week commented:

[I] found I could manage quite nicely [financially] without other children.

Whereas some case study childminders experienced difficulty in filling vacancies, other childminders said this had not been a problem. Differences between areas in supply and demand appeared to account for some of this variation:

Because a lot of the families around here, both parents are professionals – they tend to go back to work. – or the ones that don't go back to work, can afford not to go back … so there's always a shortage of minders. (new childminder)

One factor cited for a lack of business included the increasing supply of nurseries and after-school care:

I was made redundant. The local nurseries started up and there were very few children available. (ex-childminder)

Other factors included negative reports about childminding in the media which deterred parents from using childminders; and childminders themselves having specific requirements regarding the children they take, the hours they work or the fees they charge.

Those childminders, especially established childminders, who had no difficulty filling vacancies said that their children came largely through recommendation, either from parents or other childminders. New childminders seemed more likely to experience problems because they were not yet known within their community. They may therefore find it more difficult at first to break into the market. This seems even more likely given that some of the parents we interviewed wanted an

experienced childminder and preferably someone who came recommended.

Working conditions

Pay

Homeworkers comprise some of the lowest paid workers in the labour force (Felstead and Jewson, 2000). The hourly rate charged by survey childminders ranged from £1 to £4 with an average of £2.10 and gross weekly earnings averaged £103.28. The hourly rate for case study childminders ranged from £2 to £4 and the weekly rate from £50 to £120. Both survey and case study childminders considered they were low paid for their work:

I think they should recognise childminders do work hard. We should be recognised and get paid for it.

The case studies highlight that the calculation of fees was a complicated matter, affected by such factors as parents' requirements, market forces and altruism. Knowing what to charge when first starting out was a problem, usually resolved by seeking advice from other childminders or the NCMA. Fees were calculated on an hourly, daily or weekly rate and on the basis of whether care was part-time, full-time or involved drop-off or pick-up from school. A new childminder who charged a flat fee for regular hours rather than an hourly rate explained:

I just found that if you deal with £3.50 an hour for 8.30am to 5.30pm it just works out a lot of money for those parents … It wouldn't be worth them working.

Some childminders' rates were all inclusive, whilst others charged extra for food and other items. It is understandable if parents are confused by the different rates quoted and why they may query the childminder's rate, which as we shall see in Chapter Five, can be an irritation to childminders.

Fees varied according to location, some areas commanding higher rates than others depending on demand and supply:

It's just lucky or unlucky where you happen to be living, really, which isn't fair, either. You're providing the same service, so, really, everybody should get the same money. (established childminder)

Not surprisingly, childminders were well aware of the effects of the marketplace on their earnings:

You can't charge too much, because you price yourself out of the market. So you're not earning enough to be fully independent, but at the same time you can't afford to ask for more, because then you'll have no work at all. (established childminder)

Some childminders were prepared to negotiate and vary their rate according to parents' circumstances. A desire to help parents, particularly single parents, was one reason:

I like to try and help. I can remember being hard up for money. (new childminder)

Other childminders considered it wrong to ask for more than they felt they needed. An established childminder who was charging £2.00 an hour said:

I just feel I couldn't go and say to somebody, 'You will pay me £3.00 an hour'... I feel it's just sheer greed.

In other cases, childminders appeared to adjust their fees to ensure a regular income, as explained by this established childminder:

... what is the point of me taking a child on and charging the parent £100 a week, or £85 a week, knowing full well that they're not going to be able to afford that. So why don't I have a child who's going to be £60 a week, or £65 a week, and they're going to be consistently with me?

Others said they were not prepared to negotiate over their rates. They believed that lowering their rate devalued the work they did, as this new childminder illustrates:

Because I think if you ask for less than that [£4.00 an hour], it's kind of saying it's not very good care.

However, this childminder felt guilty once she had started caring for a child at this rate:

I decided I wasn't doing it for any less ... but then when I got ... he's so nice, I started feeling guilty.

This example highlights the difficulties in trying to take a business-like approach to childminding, which does not always combine easily with the close personal relationships that develop. We shall return to this issue in the next chapter.

It was clear that many case study childminders had difficulty in broaching the subject of raising fees with parents despite a contract stating when and by how much fees were to be raised. The practice of this established childminder was not uncommon:

Most probably the children I've got at the moment I probably wouldn't do it, but if I'd got new children, I would do it. I find it very difficult.

Although some childminders did not have problems in discussing financial matters, one commenting that training had definitely helped, many did find this a particularly difficult area. We consider why this might be in the following chapter. There was also the fear among some that increasing fees may result in parents looking for an alternative arrangement. This could have negative consequences for themselves, in terms of loss of income, and for the child, who may be affected by a change in their care-giver.

Hours of work

During term-time survey childminders typically worked for five days a week, but hours per week varied. On average, they provided childcare for 34 hours a week, with the most common range being 41–50 hours (33 per cent). The hours of the case study childminders varied considerably. Some were working full-time, usually from around 8.00 am to 6.00 pm, while others preferred to work part-time or not every day. A small number considered it was not good practice to offer full-time hours. An ex-childminder who minded two days a week said that working full-time was too long because:

> It's not fair on the child as well. I don't think, personally, that a child should be left that amount of hours. Full-time, every day? I don't think that's right.

Although some childminders did take children outside 'traditional' working hours the general feeling among these childminders was that they did not want to. They felt that it interfered too much with their own family: *the evenings and weekends are for my children* said one established childminder.

It was apparent from some of the case study childminders that childminding gives some women flexibility in terms of when and how they choose to work; for example, moving from full-time to part-time childminding or vice versa or combining part-time childminding with another part-time job. In fact some childminders, having returned to a job outside the home, remained registered in case they wanted to return to childminding:

> Because I was only working part-time [in an office] and I knew that there were going to be times when other people would need their children looked after … so I kept it going [registration]. In different parts of the week [we either worked or childminded].

Annual leave and sick leave

Although 95 per cent of the survey childminders took holidays, 75 per cent did not get paid. We did not ask about sick pay. There were significant differences between case study childminders in the two authorities when it came to annual leave and sick leave. In Authority B, childminders said they were not paid when they went on holiday, nor did they get paid when they were off sick. A new childminder who took two weeks annual leave said:

> You miss it because it pays the bills, basically, at the end of the week, … It's horrible, but you get used to it.

Some childminders were of the view that as self-employed people it was something one had to expect:

> Childminding isn't guaranteed, and you're self-employed now. If you were working for yourself, and you wanted a holiday, you'd have to take it and wouldn't get paid for it

... You have to think, well, there might be weeks that I don't get paid at all. That's all part and parcel of it. (new childminder)

In Authority A, childminders had contracts stating three or four weeks paid leave and five days paid sick leave. Nevertheless, contracts did not ensure they received payment:

This is where I am a disaster! I can't ask for money for holidays because I'm getting paid for something I'm not doing, and I think that's not fair. and I wouldn't ask for sick pay. (new childminder)

In reality, childminders in both authorities had had very little time off for ill health and tended to continue working unless really unwell. A loss in income, not wanting to let parents down, and feeling uncomfortable because parents would have to pay for alternative care unless also taking time off lay behind their reluctance to take time off when unwell. However, while not dismissing the problems for parents, one ex-childminder said, commenting on paid sick leave written in to contracts supplied to all childminders in her authority to use:

It is such value to bring in the sick pay ... how can you give the job your all if you are feeling dreadful?

In-service training

Around three-quarters of the survey childminders (76 per cent), had received some non-qualification training in the last three years related to their work as childminders. This is less than the EO/IDeA survey where all respondents had undertaken some non-qualification training in an equivalent time period. As can be seen from Table 3.3, training was mainly in the areas of first aid, health and safety, child protection and child development.

Table 3.3 Non-qualification training undertaken in the last three years

Course topics	%
First aid/health and safety	61.2
Child protection	33.2
Business side of childminding	25.2
Child development	24.7
Managing children's behaviour	22.3
Equal opportunities practice	18.4
Special needs	18.2
Working with parents	16.1
Working with school-age children	14.1
Assertiveness	12.6
Working with babies/toddler	10.8
None	23.9

Source: Survey data (n=461)

Note: Respondents could give more than one option so percentages exceed 100

Table 3.4 Reasons for not attending training courses

Reasons	%
Timing of courses	47.3
Lack of time	41.8
Childcare difficulties	24.7
Cost of courses	20.7
Transport difficulties	21.7
Suitable course not available	7.9
No need for further training	6.0
No difficulties experienced	19.2

Source: Survey data (n=469)

Note: Respondents could give more than one option so percentages exceed 100

Courses are usually provided by local authorities and paid for by childminders, where there is a charge.

As reported by other researchers (Moss *et al.*, 1995; Gelder, 1998), first aid and health and safety courses tended to be rated more highly by case study childminders, whilst those to do with child development were considered less relevant given their experience as parents. However, although first aid/health and safety training had been undertaken by more survey childminders, suggesting these topics were more popular, almost a quarter had undertaken a course in child development (Table 3.3.)

Case study childminders expressed differing views about the value of training in general, with some seeing it as beneficial, as this new childminder expressed:

It is relevant, because, obviously, the more you can learn, and the more you can take on board, the more you can give the children that you're looking after.

Others, such as another new childminder, thought the practical experience of parenting was of greater benefit:

At the end of the day, being a parent is the only way of learning.

Despite the less positive stance on training that some case study childminders took, only a very small proportion of the survey childminders (6 per cent) thought they needed no further training (Table 3.4).

Table 3.4 presents the difficulties survey childminders had in attending training courses, although around a fifth said that they had experienced no difficulties. Commenting on the difficulty of attending training courses, one survey childminder wrote:

Childminders should be able to attend training courses, but as a single parent with no financial support if I do not work I do not earn an income ... it is impossible for me to attend as most are run in the daytime when I am working.

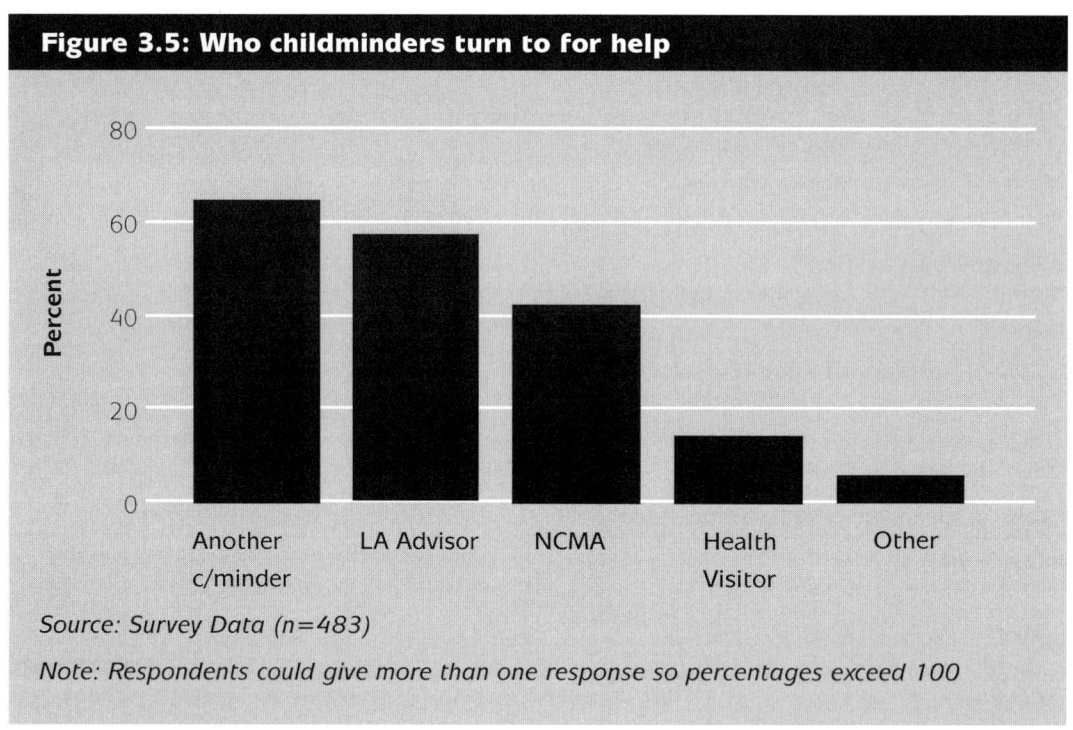

Figure 3.5: Who childminders turn to for help

Source: Survey Data (n=483)

Note: Respondents could give more than one response so percentages exceed 100

As with survey childminders, timing of courses was perceived as the biggest obstacle by case study childminders. They did not want to attend evening courses because it meant giving up time with their family or attending after a full day's work. Most would not attend day-time courses because of childcare problems:

> Parents ... they're paying me to mind their child, not for their child to be put in a crèche while I'm doing something else. (established childminder)

Clearly childminders do manage to attend training courses, but from our data there would appear to be a need to look at ways in which training can be accessed more easily.

Support

Satisfaction with their work and the quality of their childcare are associated with how well supported childminders feel they are (Molgaard, 1993: Pence and Goelman, 1991). Among the survey childminders, just over half (55 per cent) were members of the NCMA. Almost one-third (30 per cent) of the survey childminders met up with other childminders, but almost two-thirds (64 per cent) either did not meet other childminders or did so only occasionally. However, very few felt there was no one to turn to when they needed help or advice with their childminding (Figure 3.5).

As in the survey, more than half of the case study childminders referred to the support that other childminders offered them:

> We say jokingly, nobody understands a childminder like another one.

Several were members of local branches of the NCMA. They referred to the support the organisation gave them:

> I've joined the NCMA and the information

they send you is brilliant. (new childminder)

There were differences between case study childminders in the two authorities with respect to the support they received from their local authority. Authority A childminders tended to turn to their colleagues, because they felt there was little support forthcoming from the local authority:

> *I mean, to me they were supposed to be there for support, but I never felt they gave me a bit.*

Childminders in Authority B were more positive about their local authority:

> *Absolutely brilliant. Very supportive. Nice sound advice.*

Childminders in both authorities, however, felt there could be more support and advice for childminders generally.

Case study childminders were asked how supportive their family was of their work and the impact their work had on their family. Almost all said their partners had been supportive, three having themselves also registered to provide support. A minority of childminders spoke about difficulties to do with partners coming home and being irritated that they were still working. Some had to make allowances for partners who were shift-workers and trying to sleep during the day:

> *I don't think I'll take a baby on again ... if he was at work all day, it wouldn't matter.* (new childminder)

All childminders believed that childminding had benefited their own children in terms of providing company and developing their social skills.

Childminding as work

A career as a childminder

The survey data provides evidence of how committed childminders are to their work. More than half said they wanted to be childminding more than anything else (Figure 3.6). Of those who would prefer to be doing another job, the majority wanted a job working with children.

More than half saw childminding as either their chosen career (38 per cent) or as a stepping-stone to related work (15 per cent), while 41 per cent saw childminding as convenient while their children were young and still at home. Very few saw it as temporary employment (7 per cent). From this data, two groups of childminders emerge. A group who see childminding as a long-term career and a group where childminding may be more of a passing phase. From our survey data there was no way of knowing whether those who saw childminding as a long-term career saw it in the same way when they first started. Since this group had been childminding for longer, there is the possibility that length of time in the job affected perceptions of it as a career. The case studies shed more light on this issue.

Case study childminders who were new to childminding were more likely to say they would only be childminding for another three or four years or until their children were of school age. Established childminders, who on average had been working for ten years, appeared to want to continue for longer or until they retired. Four of the five childminders with a childcare qualification saw childminding and childcare as a long-term career. Of the ten who had left childminding, for example, two of the three who had

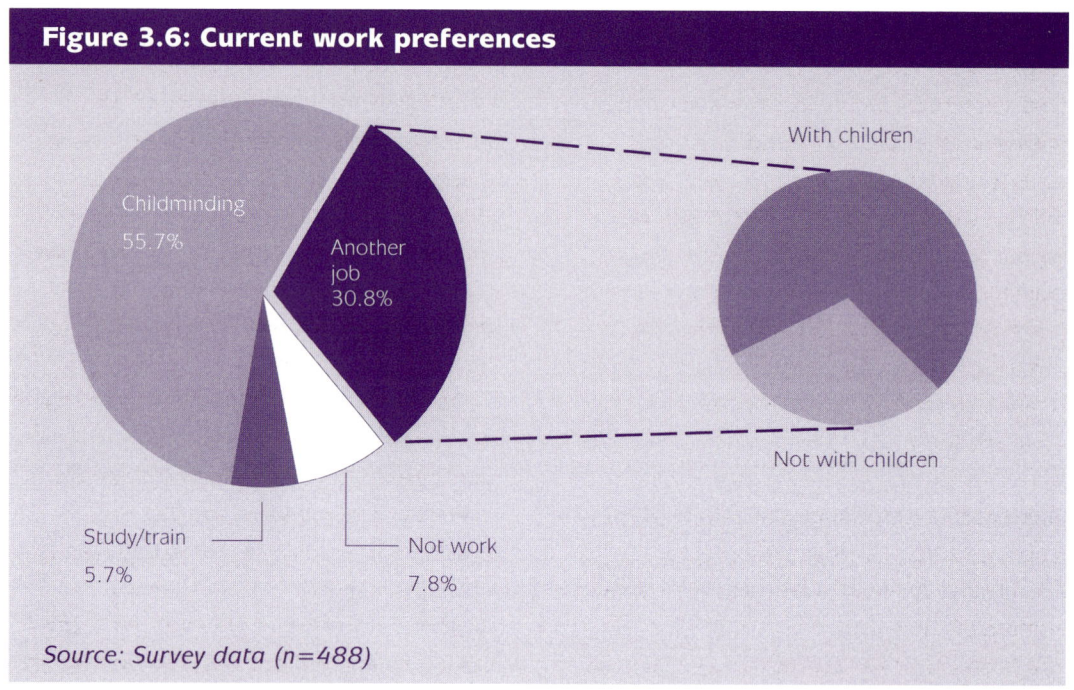

Figure 3.6: Current work preferences

Childminding 55.7%

Another job 30.8%

With children

Not with children

Study/train 5.7%

Not work 7.8%

Source: Survey data (n=488)

continued to work with children also had a childcare qualification. An ex-childminder currently working as a nanny because she had difficulty finding work as a childminder said:

> *I certainly do [see it as a career]. I see it as a vocation.*

Many of the ex-childminders and established childminders had initially viewed childminding in terms of a stop-gap in their employment career when they first started. Childminding was something they could do until their children reached school-age, as this established childminder who was planning to stop when her youngest child was of school age says:

> *Once [child] is in school, that's it. I'm shaking it off, and I'm doing something else. And it [childminding] will have been something that's got me by over the last five years.*

However, several of these childminders had continued beyond the time they had initially anticipated stopping for one or more of the following reasons:

- enjoyment of the work;
- lacking confidence in finding another job outside the home or not wanting to face the perceived stresses of another job;
- still being available for their children in times of illness or family emergencies;
- the difficulties of finding work that fitted around school hours and school holidays.

Since within our society childcare work has a low status, to which poor working conditions contribute, it may not be surprising that those working in the field may not value childcare as a career or occasionally not see it as a 'proper' job:

> *It's not that I can't be bothered to go out to work. I couldn't get a job. I really couldn't get a job.* (new childminder)

There has been some expansion of employment opportunities in the childcare field as seen, for example, by childminders moving into related careers such as development workers. Nevertheless, it is difficult for childminders to see how their experience can be valued in the wider labour market, as suggested by this childminder:

> It's not going to get you anywhere, really, is it? Apart from perhaps organising a playgroup or something like that. (new childminder)

There was also the suggestion within case study accounts that childminding could not be a career because it was very similar to being at home and caring for one's own children, which again gains little recognition within the labour market:

> I suppose it is a career in a way. I don't know. You don't really look at it – when you're doing it, you're just doing it. It's just something you do. I suppose it's like – you know, a mother at home, bringing up their children. You just do it, don't you? Because that's what – it's got to be done. (established childminder)

Childminding as home work

As with other homeworkers, childminders have to balance the demands of their work with the demands of their home and family:

> This was mainly a playroom. My sitting-room was a playroom...It wasn't my sitting-room. But we didn't think of it like that. Daytime, it was my place of work. And it was the children's room. (ex-childminder)

Huws (1994), in a survey of homeworkers whose work was under the control of an outside employer and therefore did not include childminders, reported that stress caused by the need to divide attention between work and children was their most frequent difficulty. This is likely to be less of a problem for childminders where childcare is the work they are engaged in. However, case study childminders did talk about the difficulties they sometimes faced in setting and maintaining boundaries around their work and family life. This established childminder said:

> You never really get away from your job. Whereas if you work in an office or whatever, you shut the door and come home. You've left your work behind, whereas, you know it's always here, really! But, then again, I quite like I mean, that's the only downside, I would say, from being in your own home.

Childminders have much in common, such as low pay and poor working conditions, with manual workers who work at home, as distinguished from those who work from home (eg. electricians). Very few homeworkers, however, are in the same position as childminders, whose home and immediate family members are assessed not only by official regulators, but also by the users of the service. A case study childminder sums it up thus:

> It's very difficult, because it is your home. You live here. But it's also your place of work. So they've [parents] got a certain right to see where their child's going to be. It's a fine line between balancing their right to see where their child's going to be, and your right to privacy in your own home. I mean, it's pretty unique. I mean, no other job is like that. Because most other jobs you

do at home, it's either I don't know, work on a computer which you send off, and they don't need to see where you're doing it. Or something like that. They don't need to examine your house.

Although not explored in the survey, case study childminders volunteered several advantages and disadvantages to working at home, which are very similar to those reported by homeworkers in other surveys (Huws, 1994; Phizacklea and Wolkowitz, 1995). The advantages included being available for their family, freedom to choose how to organise their work, and feeling more relaxed in their own home. The disadvantages included isolation, the cleaning and tidying-up, the wear and tear on the home, and the difficulty of trying to balance work and family life.

Summary

Most childminders in this study were women, living as a couple and with children of their own. Generally, their motivation to become a childminder was to be at home with their own children and earn an income. Consequently, these childminders tended to start childminding when they had young, pre-school children at home.

Compared with other childcare workers, childminders are less likely to have formal educational qualifications and a childcare-related qualification. Possibly because there is no requirement for childminders to be trained and qualified in childcare, training and qualifications were seen by some as less relevant to them.

Some childminders considered their experience as parents was valuable and training was important in helping them to build upon their skills. Others were of the opinion that being a parent was sufficient training for childminding. This is a view that has been challenged by the NCMA for many years. Empirical research has consistently found a significant relationship between childcare training and quality of care (see Mooney and Munton, 1997) and there are many examples presented in this chapter where training could be beneficial, such as handling difficult situations with parents. It is, therefore, important to find ways in which this group can be encouraged to accept the benefits of training.

However, poor working conditions, such as long hours, unpaid holidays and low pay, make a significant contribution to the negative attitudes towards training and qualifications expressed by some childminders. Yet, despite poor working conditions, childminders show a high commitment to their work with many seeing it as a long-term career, although they often begin childminding believing it to be a stop-gap in their employment career.

Compared with other homeworkers, childminders find themselves in a unique position with respect to the scrutiny they, their family and their home are subject to. Nevertheless, the regulation of childminding was overwhelmingly endorsed, although there was criticism of the process.

4 | How childminders see their work

Previous studies have reported that childminders see childminding as very much akin to being a mother (eg. Ferri, 1992; Nelson, 1994; Taylor *et al.,* 1999). Over recent years, through training and the work of the National Childminding Association (NCMA), childminders have been encouraged to see themselves as professionals and to take a more businesslike approach.

Steps have also been taken to advance the role of childminders in children's education. In the last 18 months a new childminding network scheme called Children Come First has been launched by the NCMA. Each network is a formal group of registered childminders who are assessed, recruited and monitored by a network co-ordinator and may be eligible for accreditation as education providers for three- and four-year-olds.

In this chapter we use our survey and case-study data to look at how childminders understand the nature of their work, what they consider their role to be and whether childminding is seen as a business. We also explore their satisfaction with what they do.

Nurse, teacher, mother? The role of a childminder

Childminders' views

We were interested in how childminders saw their role and what they thought were their objectives as childminders. Table 4.1 presents the data from the survey and shows that safety and child-centred objectives, such as making children feel loved and helping children develop and learn, were usually rated as very important. Objectives such as a service for families, preparing children for school and allowing mothers to work were less likely to be rated this highly. Around three-quarters (76 per cent) thought that providing a home away from home was a very important goal.

We saw in the previous chapter how

Table 4.1 Childminders' ratings of the importance of goals in their work

	N	No %	Importance Somewhat %	Very %
Provide safe physical environment	495	-	1.6	98.4
Make children feel loved	494	-	6.9	93.1
Help children develop and learn	492	0.2	12.2	87.6
Help child like self	488	0.8	18.9	80.2
Provide fun-filled activities	489	-	20.0	80.0
Home away from home	487	0.8	23.0	76.2
Social contacts for children	492	2.0	27.0	70.9
Service for families	491	1.6	42.2	56.2
Prepare children for school	489	2.0	45.4	52.6
Allow mothers to work	487	4.7	47.4	47.8

Source: Survey data

childminders regarded the experience of being a parent as important to their work. Much of the work they do as a childminder is similar to what they do for their own children. For example, providing a safe environment in which children feel secure, can establish close, warm relationships and wherein a variety of activities are provided to facilitate their development. It may be difficult, therefore, to differentiate the care provided as a mother from the care provided as a childminder, particularly as they both take place in the childminder's home. The case study childminders, indeed, spoke about their role as being close to being a mother and wanting to treat child-minded children like their own children or as extended members of their family. For example, a new childminder talking about a child who did not settle says:

She wasn't as much family, even though I tried hard to make her part of the family. But she just somehow never got the – I never was as relaxed as with [other child].

It seemed from some accounts that childminders did differentiate between the two roles of mother and childminder, but struggled to express the difference and talked about being 'second mums' because it was the only way they could emphasise the relationship that could develop between them and the children in their care:

You're like mum, but you're not mum – you're more like an auntie, rather than just the childminder.

Just over a third of the case study childminders said that a good childminder is characterised by being a parent and treating child-minded children in the same way as their own. The parenting styles of childminders clearly influenced the way in which they behaved with child-minded children, as this childminder talking about not moving breakable objects illustrates:

I've never moved it for my own son, I am not moving it for childminded children. They will learn not to touch. (established childminder)

You're a big part of their upbringing. So you've got to be able to talk to the parents about the child's upbringing … I don't just mean the physical things … I mean about the kind of values they want their child to learn.

Although most case study childminders did describe their role as being similar to being a mother, not all did so as this last quote illustrates. Childminders who did not describe their role in such as way were all new to childminding, which may suggest that those coming into the occupation are beginning to express their role differently. Training may have a role to play here, since two of the four childminders who did not describe their role as similar to motherhood had a childcare qualification and the other two had positive attitudes towards training and qualifications.

Whilst 88 per cent of survey childminders thought it was a very important part of their role to help children develop and learn, fewer (53 per cent) considered that preparing children for school was very important (Table 4.1). The views of the case study childminders reflect these views. Most believed they had an important role to play in children's development, particularly helping children to become independent and develop social skills. They were not all convinced, however, that they had a role to play in children's pre-school education:

You're there to provide care. You're not there to be their pre-school. (new childminder)

The opinion was expressed that childminders were not adequately trained: *Nursery teachers, they're qualified to do that. And they really know their stuff and they're so good at it and we're not nursery teachers,*

or sufficiently recompensed to take on such a role: *But we're not teachers … [if we are to become teachers] then we should get paid as a proper job.* (new childminder)

Furthermore, there were fears that if standards were set for childminders to meet educational goals, childminders might move towards a more formalised approach and away from an informal, learning through play approach favoured by early years specialists.

Parents' views

Few parents were expecting childminders to be a substitute parent, but they were looking for a happy, loving environment (Table 4.2).

Neither were many parents wanting childminders to prepare their child for nursery/school, though they did expect that they should be developing children's social skills, which itself is a very important preparation for nursery/school. Asked specifically if childminders should have an educational role, all parents implied that childminders should be helping children learn through play, but fewer parents (eight) believed that they should be fulfilling a role similar to that of a nursery teacher.

Views of registration and inspection staff

Although we did not interview registration and inspection staff, there was a suggestion in some of the childminder interviews that there may be significant differences between how the role is perceived by the two groups. Childminders often want the childminded children to fit into their family routines. They want to carry on in much the same way as they would with their own children. Registration and inspection staff, on the other hand, do not necessarily see this as always appropriate. They believe that a childminder's

Table 4.2 What parents want from their childminder

	N
Caring environment where child is happy	14
Develop children's social skills	12
Substitute parent	5
Stimulating environment	4
Safe environment	3
Preparation for nursery/school	2

Source: Parent telephone interviews (n=21)

Note: Parents could give more than one response so number exceeds 21

attention should be focused at all times on the children, as this childminder suggests:

> I'm supposed to be playing with her [minded child], doing everything with her, and listening and taking in everything that she's saying to me. And no one can do that. (new childminder)

Such differences in how the role is perceived may account for some of the tensions arising between childminders and registration and inspection staff as described in Chapter Three.

A good childminder

Case study childminders were asked what makes a good childminder. Over half referred to characteristics of the childminder, such as communication skills, ability to set boundaries, and a sense of humour, but the most frequently-mentioned characteristic was patience. This was the characteristic most frequently mentioned by parents, too. We did not probe what it meant to be patient, although Nelson (1994), using a definition provided from one of her interviewees in the United States, suggests that it may be particularly complex, 'patience is understanding the individuality of all of these children' (page190).

This view is supported by other research. In an Australian survey of 53 family day-care providers, a third highlighted patience as an important characteristic (Clyde and Rodd, 1994). The researchers claim that childcare providers 'mean patience to be the selection of a more tolerant, developmentally appropriate and reflective response, rather than the dictionary definition of suffering and endurance' (p39).

Liking children and caring about them were also important characteristics mentioned

by both childminders and parents. Many parents and childminders were of the opinion that a good childminder would not be motivated by financial reasons, but primarily because they liked children:

> A good childminder has to love children, and not just do it for the money. (ex-childminder)

Vincent and Ball (1999) also found in interviews with parents that there was disapproval of child-carers who appeared to be more motivated by money than the care of children. Case study childminders were particularly critical of other childminders who appeared to put money before children:

> She's bringing in far too many children to actually be able to look after properly. Just to earn more money. That's wrong. Because then it's not about childcare, is it? It's about the money going in your pocket, and who cares about what's happening to the children? (ex-childminder)

In fact, as described in the previous chapter, many childminders chose not to care for the number of children they were registered for, often because they felt this jeopardised the quality of care they could offer.

Childminding as a business

Like Ferri (1992), we too found that among case study childminders there was a tension between being committed to childcare and wanting to earn a reasonable income from it. Just over half the case study childminders said they did see childminding as a business.

Among childminders who did not see childminding as a business, there was a fear that were it to be viewed in such a way, one's primary concern would be about finances and not about children. For these childminders, childcare is seen in terms of the love and enjoyment of childcare and this is incompatible with a focus on money:

> I see it more as a job that I'm doing. That's my job. But it's rewarding, and I enjoy it. Otherwise I wouldn't, if I was looking at it on the business side, no … If I was looking at it that way, I'd prefer to go out to work – Tesco's, or work in an office. (established childminder)

The fact that childminders and parents come to know each other well, and the relationship is often one of mutual trust, clearly changes the perception of childminding as a business. Many said they started out thinking of it in this way, but over time their thinking had changed. One childminder who was active within her local branch of the NCMA said that although childminders should see it as a business, she found it difficult to do so. Not only did getting to know parents change perceptions of it as a

business, but working from home also had an effect:

> Where at the same time you've got the children you might do a bit of dusting or something … it's awkward. (established childminder)

The fact that childminders considered childminding to be similar to raising a family precluded some childminders from seeing it in terms of work, as this childminder illustrates:

> I don't really treat it as work, as such, to me. It's just they're part of the family unit when they're here. And I just treat them as part of a family. (established childminder)

The group who saw childminding as a business appeared no less caring. Probably there was a greater recognition among them that what they did could be viewed in this way and not detract from caring about children. For example, two childminders who worked together and who saw it very much as a

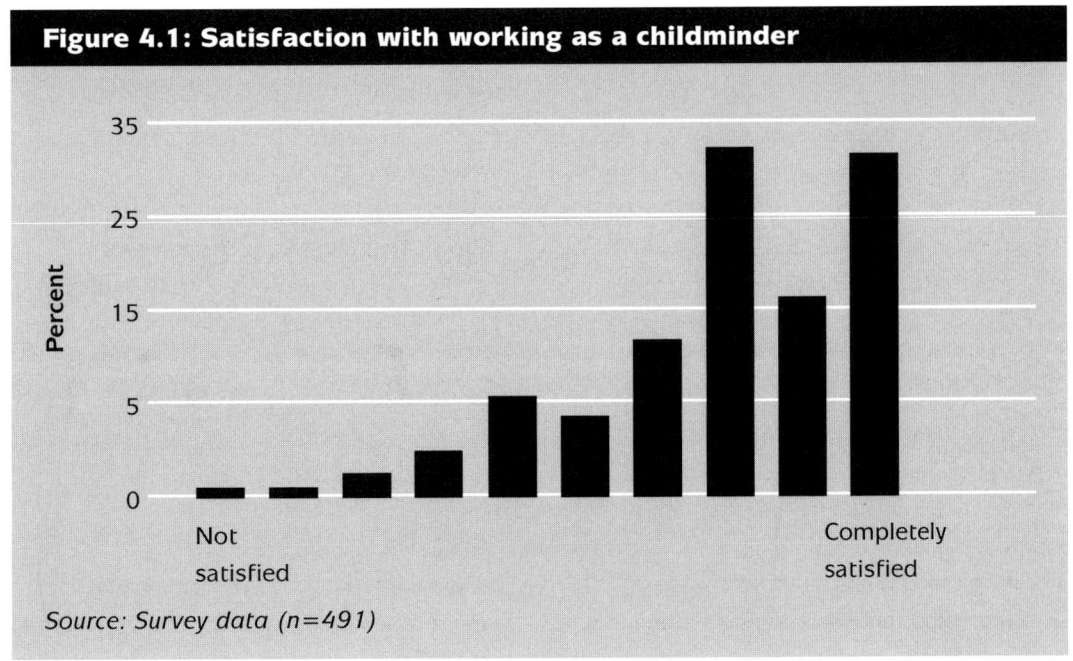

Figure 4.1: Satisfaction with working as a childminder

Source: Survey data (n=491)

business were proud of the work they did and found it rewarding. Another childminder, who had to make a decision as to which arrangement she discontinued when she found she could not manage the two children she was minding, explained:

> If your emotions ruled your head – you know, if your heart ruled your head, you wouldn't get anywhere, would you? You have to treat it as a business ... And I had more money from [child]. Simple as that. (new childminder).

Others referred to tax returns, regulations, being self-employed and wanting to be more professional as reasons why they saw childminding as a business. A childminder who emphasised the professional aspect to seeing childminding as a business said:

> A friendship element does come into it, because of the amount of contact you have and I actually quite like them as people. But it has to stay fairly professional, because they're paying me to do a service, after all.

> They're paying you to look after their child. You're being paid to do a job. (new childminder)

Satisfaction with their work

In analysis of the British Household Panel Study, childcare workers have been found to be among those groups of workers most satisfied with their job (Rose, 1999). Our sample of childminders, indeed, recorded a high level of satisfaction with childminding, despite long hours and low pay (Figure 4.1). Using a ten point scale, fewer than one in five recorded a satisfaction rating of five or less.

When asked to choose just one aspect that they liked most about being a childminder, being able to combine paid work with being at home was chosen by more childminders (27 per cent) than anything else (see Table 4.3). As one childminder explained:

> Childminding is an excellent job for a parent who wishes to stay at home with their own children yet still contribute to the family budget.

Table 4.3 What childminders find most satisfying about childminding

	%
Combining paid work with being at home	27.0
The challenge of caring for young children	15.0
Affection children show you	14.6
Being needed by the children	12.6
Using your skills in the best possible way	10.8
Working as a professional childcare worker	8.7
Fulfilling your chosen career	3.0
Being able to set your own work schedule	3.0
The appreciation shown by parents	1.8
Being able to make decisions on your own	0.6
Other reason	2.6

Source: Survey data (N=492)

Table 4.4 What childminders find most dissatisfying about childminding

	%
Society's lack of recognition for your work	39.7
Making less money than you feel you deserve	16.9
Lack of appreciation from parents	12.2
Having to juggle conflicting tasks or duties	6.5
Difficulty in filling vacancies	6.3
The effect it has on your own family	5.7
A child crying or whining a lot	2.6
Lack of professional development	2.4
Clearing up after children	2.2
Lack of support from agencies/professionals	0.8
Other reason	4.5

Source: Survey data (N=491)

Case study childminders, too, derived much pleasure and satisfaction from their work mirroring the satisfaction expressed by survey childminders:

You just can't better it;
It's hard work, but it's rewarding;
I love my job.

Much of their satisfaction came from finding children enjoyable to be with and having a role in their development. Other aspects that were particularly liked about the work included developing social networks, their availability for their family, the flexibility and freedom of the work, and parents showing their appreciation.

When asked to choose one aspect about childminding they most disliked, by far the most frequent response in the survey was society's lack of recognition for the work they did, followed by earning less than they thought they deserved and lack of appreciation from parents (see Table 4.4).

Case study childminders, too, were dissatisfied with the lack of recognition for their work and how it is devalued in our society. Their anger was expressed in a number of ways. One childminder recalled how she had been told by her building society that childminding did not count as an occupation. The fact that all childcare tends to be devalued did not escape the attention of this childminder:

You can do without so many people, but you can't do without childcare. And you need good childcare. ... It's very undervalued. As housewives are. Anyone that takes care of children. People seem to think that anyone can do it. Well, if anyone can do it, how come we have so many dysfunctional children? (ex-childminder)

Others described how they received veiled derision when responding to questioning about what they did:

*And it's always that 'Oh, aren't you
wonderful? I couldn't do that'. It's that sort
of hidden feeling – I don't think you'd want
to. And, 'if you were a bit brighter, you'd be
doing a proper job'. So I picked up a lot of
that.* (ex-childminder)

It is not surprising that in doing a job that is so
devalued, childminders themselves find they
talk about it disparagingly, as some explained:
*People are going 'Oh, I'm only a
childminder', and I'd say, 'No. I'm a
childminder. Not **only** a childminder'.
Because you don't want to put yourself
down. That is your job.* (ex-childminder)

Both groups of childminders (survey and case
studies) put forward suggestions as to how
the status of childminding could be enhanced.
Among survey respondents, three-quarters
(75%) felt that positive publicity was needed
about childminding, ahead of better pay
(62%), financial support from the Government
(57%) and the provision of a professional
qualification (50%). Childminders who made
additional comments clearly felt strongly
about this issue:
*I wish the general public would recognise
that childminding is a proper job ... All
through my career I have been asked
'Wouldn't you prefer to do a proper job?'
and of course I do. The Government could
do much to improve childminder's credibility
by positive press and government training
courses [which are] universally recognised.*

With respect to a recognised qualification for
childminding, childminders will now have
access to the new Certificate in Childminding
Practice following the launch of this award by
the Council for Awards in Children's Care and

Education (CACHE). The Certificate will be
offered through colleges and other CACHE
centres such as NCMA.

Additional suggestions put forward to
improve the status of childminding included:
* better information to users and providers
  about a childminder's role;
* changing the name to reflect what
  childminders do, *'We don't just mind the
  child'*;
* raising standards.

The majority of case study childminders
asserted that they would recommend
childminding as a job to somebody else, in
fact many had done so. This perhaps confirms
their overall satisfaction with the work.
However, their recommendation was not
unqualified:
*I think you've got to be the right type of
person.*

The right person was someone who had
experience of children or being at home with
young children, was organised, patient and,
for one childminder, able to recognise that
children have different needs. Again, as we
have seen in the definition of a good
childminder, the person should be motivated
by love of children:
*As long as they understood that it's caring
for a child. It's not making money.* (ex-
childminder)

Summary

Childminders describe their role as being very
similar to that of a mother. This seemed, in
some cases, to be because it was difficult to
articulate the difference between childminder
and mother, especially since the roles are very

similar in terms of what childminders do for both their own children and child-minded children.

Childminders believe they play an important part in children's development and learning, but are less certain about the role they have in children's education. This may be due to a misunderstanding of what education means for young children, which is something that could be addressed in training.

However, concern was voiced about formalising the educational role of childminders, which they thought might result in childminders moving away from a learning through play approach. Again, training can help childminders to understand that this does not have to be the case, as evidenced by approved childminding networks, which deliver nursery education.

Good childminders were seen by both childminders and parents to be patient, which may mean taking a tolerant approach which matches the needs of children. Good childminders were also perceived as being primarily motivated by wanting to be with children rather than the need for an income. For some childminders this may make it difficult to see childminding as a business and take a business-like approach to their work.

Finally, childminders derived much satisfaction from their work. Much of their satisfaction came from being with children and knowing that they were helping in their development. The greatest source of dissatisfaction was the way in which their work was devalued and the poor image that childminding has within our society.

5 | Childminders and parents

Several studies, both here and abroad, have shown that one of the reasons that women enter childminding is because they do not want to place their own children in childcare (Mayall and Petrie, 1983; Nelson, 1989; Saggers *et al.*, 1994). Furthermore, childminders are unlikely to endorse mothers returning to work when their children are young (Ferri, 1992; Nelson, 1989). However, these studies were conducted before the recent significant increase in the number of working mothers with young children and attitudes may have changed.

Although there is research that has looked at the relationship between parents and childminders (eg. Ferri, 1992; Nelson, 1989), there is little that is recent. The conclusion from this research suggests that the 'straddling of private and public boundaries' inherent within the childminding arrangement can create ambiguity of roles and conflict within the relationship.

Using results from the survey, case studies and parent interviews, this chapter addresses childminders' attitudes towards non-parental employment, use of non-parental childcare, issues around making the childcare arrangement and relationships between childminder and parent.

Attitudes towards non-parental childcare

Working mothers

Childminders, as with other childcare providers, most often care for children whose parents are working. Since many childminders become childminders so that they can be at home with their children, we were particularly interested in their views about working mothers.

Before becoming childminders, almost a third of the survey childminders (31 per cent) had left their children in someone else's care while they were at work. Friends and relatives were the most frequently used form of childcare (43 per cent) followed by childminders (26 per cent) and a spouse/ partner (22 per cent). A similar picture emerged for the case studies regarding the use of childcare.

As can be seen from Table 5.1, childminders' acceptance of mothers working, if they so choose, increases with the child's

Table 5.1 Views on whether mothers should work, by age of child				
	N	Not work %	Work p/t only %	Work p/t or f/t %
Under 12 months	476	17.0	31.1	51.9
12 to 35 months	469	7.7	25.2	67.2
36 months to school entry	468	3.2	19.9	76.9
School entry age to eight	466	0.4	10.3	89.3
From eight to end of primary	468	0.2	7.5	92.3
Secondary school age	468	-	3.8	96.2
Source: Survey data				

age. Whereas almost all think it is acceptable when a child is over the age of eight, only around a half consider it acceptable with a child under a year old. This compares with female respondents in the 1994 British Social Attitudes Survey, where only 5 per cent thought it acceptable for mothers to work full-time with a child under five (Thomson, 1996).

Conditional acceptance

The majority view was not one of explicit disapproval of working mothers, as the quote from this established childminder shows:

They've got to earn a living the same as I earn a living. If I didn't have their children, then I wouldn't be working, would I? Yeah, I think a lot more women are going back to work, and I think it's good. A lot of them have good careers that they follow. And a lot of them then work around their children, and try and do the best they can.

This childminder accepts the different reasons why women with young children may return to work, but not all case study childminders took this view.

A quarter expressed implied criticism of women who returned to work from choice rather than necessity:

Fine, I had to do it. It's part of necessity these days, isn't it ... And I just thought, you don't have to go back to work ... To me, people like that don't need to do it. (new childminder)

Perhaps this lack of understanding has its roots in the fact that many of these childminders are working because of financial necessity and, given a choice, would prefer not to work while their children are young.

One childminder who was explaining she knew through experience how difficult it was to leave a baby, went on to say:

If they're having to because of the money, then it's often harder for them to leave their children than if they're going back to a job they really enjoy, and are choosing to.

Thus, some childminders distinguish differences in parental behaviour in terms of the reasons why mothers are returning to work. It would seem that childminder training has an important role to play in facilitating discussion and challenging such views.

Affect on parents and children

It was not unusual for case study childminders to say that parents, and sometimes children, are missing out because mothers are working. For this childminder, who would not have left her own children, the child must be feeling rejected and missing maternal love:

And I think it's very sad, because a child's been sent out to somewhere ... Mum's out working, and he needs a comfortable environment – to feel he's cared for and loved.

Occasionally, childminders felt that children received insufficient attention because their parents were working full-time. Others believe that mothers, though it would appear not fathers, miss seeing their children grow and develop:

You're missing all the best times. Little things like if they've learnt to walk in your house or learnt to do something.

Some childminders attributed parents' and childrens' behaviour to the fact that mothers worked. A childminder trying to understand a child's extremely disruptive behaviour said:

From three months old he was in day care.
She never had him with her. He's always
been looked after by other people, and
could it just be a little rebellion against his
mum always leaving him? … I think he just
really needed his mum and lots of love.

Distress and misbehaviour were sometimes described as expressions of children missing their mums, whereas maternal guilt about working explained why some mothers, in the opinion of their childminder, were too lenient or possessive with their children.

The view that children, when they are young, should be in the exclusive care of their mothers would appear to be influencing these attitudes towards working mothers. This ideology has dominated for many years (Mooney and Munton, 1997) and remains influential despite the increasing numbers of mothers with young children now in the workforce. There is evidence that within the childcare workforce, childminders are not alone in holding such views. Reservations about women with younger children working are also found amongst other childcare workers. Very few students on childcare courses expressed a preference to work full-time if they had a pre-school child (Cameron *et al.,* forthcoming). Almost half preferred to work part-time followed by not working or working from home. Many believed it important for mothers to be available for their children during the school day or at home after school hours.

Views on different types of childcare

Perhaps not surprisingly, childminders see themselves as the best type of non-parental childcare for all ages of children, but especially for children aged under three. For infants under one, survey childminders said the best type of care was either a childminder (68 per cent) or a relative (25 per cent). For children aged between one and three, 82 per cent chose childminders and 11 per cent relatives.

Case study childminders felt that they were able to give children more attention and provide a home-like environment. Because of higher ratios and larger groups they could not see how children in nurseries could get the same level of individual attention. One childminder who had worked in a nursery observed:

It was very hard to comfort a child when
there was about four staff to eighteen
babies at one point. (established
childminder)

Experience as mothers was also seen as an advantage that childminders could offer:

They get a more motherly attention from
someone that has been a mother that's got
her own children – rather than someone,
say, a young girl that's just gone into doing
childcare. (ex-childminder)

Childminders were not in favour of nurseries for children under the age of three. Just one childminder considered nurseries the best childcare for infants and only 22 (5 per cent) thought nurseries were the best type of childcare for one- to three-year-olds.

Two childminders referred to the fact that there were other adults in the nursery to provide back-up for one another as one of the benefits of group care.

Making the arrangement

Choosing a childminder

We asked the 21 parents we interviewed why they had chosen to use a childminder. Almost a half mentioned affordability and the same number mentioned individual attention or a home like environment. Other reasons were location, flexibility of hours and unavailability of other forms of care. For more than half, a childminder was their preferred choice when they were first looking for childcare. For the remainder, reasons of affordability or availability were given as to why they could not use the type of childcare they would have liked, usually a nanny or group care.

When asked what they were looking for when choosing a childminder, parents listed a number of characteristics, although as can be seen from Table 5.2, features of the environment and personal qualities of the childminder were most frequently mentioned. In response to this question parents often made comments such as:

Somewhere where my child will be happy.

Only a third of parents believed that a childcare qualification was important for childminders. About half thought it was more important for childminders to be parents or have experience of children.

Although parents were saying that cost was a significant factor in their choice of childcare, and childminders had often found childcare too expensive when they themselves were using it, some childminders were disconcerted when parents focused on costs or quibbled about fees:

You're quoting a reasonable amount, but the reaction was shock, horror. 'Can you go down a little bit lower than that?' And I'd always say 'no' ... It's a big responsibility, isn't it, looking after other people's children. And to be so unappreciated before you've even started looking after their children is just not on. (ex-childminder)

Of course, childminders are coming from the viewpoint that the valuable work they do is not fully recognised and commands a low reward in financial terms. Perhaps this explains

Table 5.2 What parents look for when choosing a childminder

	N
Personal qualities of childminder	12
Environment	11
Age and presence of other children	8
Experience	6
Flexibility	4
Location or cost	4
Variety of activities	3
Professional attitude	3
Similar ethnic background to parent	2

Source: Parent telephone interviews (n=21)

Note: Respondents could give more than one response so number exceeds 21

why they might feel aggrieved when parents want to negotiate a lower rate.

Finding a childminder

Apart from one parent who was a student, the remaining 20 parents were using childcare because they were working. Thirteen parents had found their childminder from the list provided by their local authority. In four of these cases the parents' decision was influenced by realising they already knew the childminder or a friend of theirs did. Five found their childminder through personal recommendation and three through an advertisement. Although for one parent the process of finding someone took four months, the majority had found someone suitable within two to four weeks. Many parents said they had contacted several childminders, in some cases as many as 20, to find that few had vacancies.

Nine parents had not visited childminders other than the one they placed their child with. Reasons for not doing so included: no other childminders with vacancies, no time because the previous arrangement had ended with little notice, the childminder was recommended. All but two parents felt that improvements could be made in the process of looking for a childminder. Suggestions included references from parents who had used the childminder, better information about which childminders had vacancies and a statement written by childminders about their service.

The 21 parents between them had 27 children within the age range 0–14 years. Twenty-five of these children were being looked after by the case study childminders. The youngest was six months and the eldest was ten years. The hours they were with their childminder varied from 3 to 55 hours per week, with an average of 28 hours per week. Three-fifths of the children had experienced another childcare provider before their current one. Reasons for changes included the childminder having stopped childminding or moving, parents unhappy with the standard of care and the arrangement being only temporary. Of the 15 children who had been in another arrangement, four had experienced three or more providers over a period averaging four years. Since stability of day-care arrangement has been associated with positive experiences for young children (Whitebook, Howes and Phillips, 1989; Martin and Plewis, 1991) this is a worrying result.

First meeting

Many childminders talked about feeling nervous or apprehensive about the first meeting with parents, particularly when they were new to childminding and had little experience:

Nerve-racking. Having two completely strange people in your house ... judging you. (new childminder)

One childminder acknowledged that parents were feeling the same way:

But they were in the same boat on the other side, I knew they were nervous as much as I was. (ex-childminder)

During the meeting, both parents and childminders are making judgements about one another and trying to decide whether an arrangement could work. Both childminders and parents felt that more could be done to help parents. Almost a third of the parents we interviewed felt that they needed more support and guidance from the local authority when looking for a childminder.

Both childminders and parents may find it difficult to say to one another that they do not think they are suited. In fact, one childminder suggested that some parents are surprised when childminders do articulate this view:

I think I offended one woman because I said 'no', because I think she felt that all the rights were with the parent about choosing a childminder. She didn't feel that the childminder had any right to decline to work for her. (new childminder)

This parent's attitude has much to do with how childminding as an occupation is understood, a point we shall return to later in this chapter.

Making a decision

Just as parents are trying to find the best arrangement for them and their child, so childminders too are trying to find an arrangement that will work for them. For example, one childminder preferred to care for babies because, thinking in the long term, the placement could potentially last longer than with an older pre-school child who may be going to school within a year or two.

Childminders consider the age of the child, the hours the parent wants childcare for, and whether caring for the child will fit into the needs of both her own family and the other minded children:

[The] childminder has to be just as selective with the family as the family is with the childminder. You get a family or a child that doesn't fit in, it has repercussions on the whole group. (ex-childminder)

Childminders also make judgements as to how well they think they will be able to get along with parents:

You've got to make sure they like you, and you like them. And because if you don't get on with the parents, there's no point in having the children. Because you're going to clash over them. (new childminder)

Childminders are also trying to judge the extent to which a parent's expectations of the arrangement correspond with what they are able to offer:

That's why it took so long to find the right family to work with, as it were. Because the family's got to want the same kind of things for a child as you're prepared to offer them. (new childminder)

Several childminders said they preferred parents that appeared easy-going and not too demanding, avoiding parents who to them seemed over-protective and fussy, because from their experience these parents were more difficult to work with:

I think, no this isn't going to work because it's just too much of a demand. There's just too many things she's asking for, and I couldn't possibly fulfil those. (established childminder)

Attempting to make such judgements on the basis of one or two meetings is extremely difficult. It is, perhaps, not then surprising that childminders talked about relying on instinct, a 'gut-feeling':

You just have a feeling. You just seem to know. Something just clicks.

Parents, too, are making judgements about the childminder and they, too, sometimes rate intuition as important in making a choice.

Although most childminders did appear to be weighing-up a number of factors in deciding whether to offer their service, not all were. At least three said that they left the decision to parents. One childminder gave the impression that she could not afford to be selective:

> I don't decide what children. I take what there is. (new childminder)

Nevertheless, it is clear that among this sample of childminders, many do place restrictions and boundaries upon their service, which, as Ferri (1992) has said, is perfectly reasonable and understandable from the childminder's perspective. However, from a parental perspective the supply of childcare provision available to them may be further reduced.

Parental satisfaction with the arrangement

All the parents we spoke to expressed satisfaction with their childminding arrangement. Two-thirds mentioned that they appreciated their childminder's flexibility. Other aspects mentioned were the opportunities their child had for socialisation, the range of activities offered by the childminder, and the relationship the childminder had with their child. Six parents referred specifically to their relationship with the childminder and aspects that they liked about it, including support, good communication, businesslike and friendly. Eight parents expressed some dissatisfaction, usually about paying the childminder when the child was not there. Of the 21 parents interviewed all but two said they would recommend childminding to other parents looking for childcare. However, many parents added the proviso that it was important for parents to find the 'right' person.

Relationships with parents

Close personal relationships

The success of the childminding arrangement appears to rest largely on the personal relationship between childminder and parents. When reaching a decision about an arrangement childminders said how important it was to feel comfortable with parents. Many said they wanted to have a good relationship so that both parties could communicate easily with one another. In talking about the sort of relationship they liked to have, case study childminders either emphasised a business relationship, a personal friendship or a combination of the two. Those emphasising friendship said that it was easier for parents to raise concerns, whilst the opposite view was taken by others who said that friendship would make this harder:

> When you're working for somebody, you can't be friends and look after their child at the same time ... And so it's always been kept a kind of business and nothing else. (new childminder)

Childminders who wanted to combine a friendly and businesslike relationship felt that familiarity led to exploitation:

> Because once they start treating you like a good friend, then I feel that's when they start taking more advantage of you. (new childminder)

One ex-childminder, acknowledging how difficult it was to achieve a balance between being friendly and businesslike, said:

> I think you kind of start off more formal than you would. And then you can lighten up ... But if you were too friendly, it was very hard to go the other way.

These childminders would appear to be articulating the difficulty of negotiating a relationship which is governed by both the norms of social exchange and the norms of a business transaction (Nelson, 1989, Vincent and Ball, 1999). As Ferri (1992) summarises, 'the complexity lies partly in the conflicting components of a relationship which requires the formality associated with financial and contractual exchanges, and, at the same time, the personal intimate rapport deemed essential in caring for a child'.

What makes the situation unique, and distinguishes it from other workers in the childcare field and the broader field of social care, is that the transactions occur in the provider's home rather than an institution or in the home of the client. In the context of group care, for example, the relationship between provider and parent may to some extent be regulated by the institutional context where there is usually a management structure which deals with problems. This can serve to avoid difficult relationships or areas of tension arising between parents and staff working directly with their children. It was encouraging to find that most case study childminders and parents expressed positive views about their relationship. However, this is not to suggest that problems had not been encountered in the past.

Conflict within the relationship

Time and again case study childminders recalled incidents which had caused tension in their relationship with parents. The few who had experienced little, if any, difficulty put it down to luck:

> I didn't have any problems. I mean, maybe I was lucky. (ex-childminder)

or the fact that they were willing to be flexible:

> I've been really, really lucky, but I think that's because I'm flexible as well. (new childminder)

Conflict tended to arise most frequently around time-keeping, payment, sick children and a feeling of being 'taken for granted'. In some instances such conflict could lead to the arrangement ending as was the case with this childminder when a parent continually arrived late to collect her child:

> We ended the contract between each other because she didn't want to pay the overtime rate. (established childminder)

Childminders were critical of parents who arrived late without prior notification, failed to realise there were other children who they had to consider and expected them to do extra hours at short notice:

> I think it was slightly sometimes being taken for granted. That it wouldn't matter if they were late, because you were at home anyway, and, 'oh, can you do me a favour and do this?' And somehow you weren't expected to have a life of your own. (ex-childminder)

Overtime rates were sometimes applied as an incentive to parents to arrive on time:

> I thought that was the only way to make them come on time, so I charged double time (ex-childminder).

Payment was another area that could cause contention. Not paying on time, cheques that bounced, not paying agreed overtime rates and not wanting to pay when the child was sick or on holiday, were some of the difficulties that case study childminders had encountered. Some parents could not accept why they should pay when the child did not go to the childminder:

> Childminders are self-employed … other self-employed people don't get paid when they are not working.

Childminders provided several reasons why parents took this attitude, including some parents not regarding childminding as an occupation and often failing to realise that the childminder's income is important to them. As one childminder explained when talking about parents suddenly announcing they were reducing their hours the following week:

> It's only a couple of pounds an hour, but it makes such a difference … but even when you've got quite close to people, it was hard to get across that, well, actually I was banking on that tenner. (ex-childminder)

A childminder who had experienced parents who were not paying on time had introduced payment in advance, but her comment illustrates how childminders often face a difficult dilemma:

> They turned up with the child, and they didn't pay and then when they did then it was like 'can I pay you half now?' And for the child's sake, I just continued … I'm more inclined to think of the child because once they're settled I don't want to disrupt them. (established childminder)

The third area causing difficulty was the care of sick children. Childminders spoke of parents being selfish and uncaring when they brought sick children:

> But to me you don't leave a sick child. It needs to be with its mother. It's better off at home. (ex-childminder)

However, some childminders although not condoning the behaviour, recognised the dilemma that parents faced when confronted by unsympathetic employers:

> Companies don't understand women having children these days, which is disgusting. (established childminder)

Another childminder, who had herself used a childminder, said that parents needed to know that:

> They'll [childminder] always be there, even if the child's not really well … Otherwise you've got to take a day off every five minutes. It's very important. You can't work unless you've got that. (ex-childminder)

Childminders whose parents showed their appreciation for what they did were less likely to feel taken for granted or exploited:

> They take advantage. You know, they'll come late. And I suppose it's been my fault. I've never said 'Oh, you owe me overtime'. If someone turns up and said to me, 'there's a bunch of flowers, thanks for the other week for working', that suits me. As long as you're appreciated, you're not used. (established childminder)

Whether self-employed or not, workers seek some feedback about how well they are doing in their job. Childminders look to parents to provide positive reinforcement and recognition for a job well done. Parents, however, may not feel that this is part of their role and it would be particularly difficult where parents may not be entirely satisfied with the arrangement.

Control

Although childminding is subject to greater regulation than was the case before the Children Act 1989, it is still very much a private arrangement between parent and provider. Consequently, it is largely left to them to decide what their respective role and relationship will be. It is a credit to both childminders and parents that so many arrangements are successful given the circumstances in which childminding takes place. Childminders spoke about the close relationship that had developed between themselves and some of their parents and how, many years later, they were still in touch with one another. Childminders also described the close relationships that developed with the children they cared for and the feeling of loss and sadness that often occurred when they left.

However, both in this and the previous chapter we have seen that the perspectives of parents and childminders can differ significantly and that these differences can be the cause of tension within the relationship. Although most of the case study childminders used contracts, which were drawn up together with parents and could be enforced, the relationship may not necessarily be perceived as equal. Childminders are aware that parents can withdraw their child, which not only affects their income, but also the child and their relationship with him/her. They are also faced with the same consequences if they terminate the arrangement. Parents, on the other hand, can feel powerless too, fearing that if they raise any problems it may have a detrimental affect on their child (Mooney and Munton, 1998). This situation may be exacerbated because the childminder is working within her own home and sometimes has more experience of childcare than the parent (Nelson, 1989). The way in which childminders in our study spoke about the tensions within the relationships they have had with parents, suggests that parents and childminders are struggling to exert some sort of control over the arrangement, albeit at a subconscious level.

Summary

A third of the survey childminders had used non-maternal childcare when they were employed in other work before childminding. Just over half felt it was appropriate for mothers with a child under a year to work, but this rose to 89 per cent when a child had reached school age. Around a third of the case study childminders, more especially new childminders, had worked outside the home and left their children in the care of someone else. There was a greater acceptance among case study childminders of mothers who worked from financial necessity rather than from choice. Both survey and case study childminders held the opinion that childminders offered the best type of childcare because they could offer more individual attention in a home setting.

Both childminders and parents are trying to find the best arrangement to meet their needs. The process can be a difficult one and it was felt that parents would benefit from more help in finding a childminder. Case study childminders articulated the difficulties in establishing a satisfactory relationship with parents, which encompassed both social and business exchanges. Nevertheless, parents and childminders generally voiced high levels of satisfaction with their current arrangements. Difficulties tended to be around time keeping, payment and sick children. Although having contracts, childminders could be faced with a difficult choice if a parent kept breaking the contractual agreement, since terminating the arrangement could have negative consequences not only for themselves in terms of income loss and loosing a child with whom they had developed a close relationship, but for the child too who could be affected by a change in their care-giver.

6 | Declining numbers of childminders

We saw in Chapter Two how the number of registered childminders has been falling steadily since 1996. At a time when the Government wants to expand childcare provision under the National Childcare Strategy, this is a worrying trend. To investigate the decrease in childminder numbers different approaches were adopted. We met with key workers, such as registration and inspection officers, childminding development workers and early years and childcare managers, in ten local authorities showing a significant fall in the number of childminders between 1997 and 1999. The sample included Inner and Outer London, Metropolitan, Unitary and Two-Tier authorities in different parts of the country. We also met with representatives of the National Childminding Association (NCMA) and conducted a postal survey of EYDCPs (details of the survey can be found in Chapter One). Participants were clearly concerned about the falling childminder numbers and wanted to contribute to a better understanding of why it was happening. Analysis of official government statistics to see if changes in other types of provision was related to the drop in childminder numbers was also undertaken. In this chapter, in addition to using the data from these different approaches, we also use data from the survey and case studies in the main study.

Statistics on childminder numbers

Between 1996 and 2000, official government statistics show a fall in the number of registered childminders, down from 109,200 to 75,600 (DoH, 1997; DfEE, 2000). Both the NCMA and the local authorities confirmed the drop in numbers. Although there is little change in NCMA membership as a proportion of the number of registered childminders, their records show a similar drop in membership over the last five years, reflecting the fall in the national figures.

All ten local authorities confirmed a decline in their childminder numbers over recent years, although it was not always possible to check the accuracy of their figures because few authorities had reliable databases before 1999. Many were using manual systems. One possibility we explored with local authorities was whether the introduction of more efficient record systems had resulted in a fall in numbers as records were brought up-to-date. Only one authority considered the fall in numbers was due to introducing a new computerised database, which no longer showed people as remaining registered when they were not.

What is going on?

We were interested in trying to understand why there was a fall in childminder numbers. Was it because there was less initial interest in childminding, fewer applicants now achieving registration, increased turnover or a combination of these factors? From initial enquiry to registration as a childminder involves a number of steps, which can vary between authorities. For example, one authority requires prospective childminders to attend a pre-registration course and have a home visit from a registration officer before making an application, whilst another invites applications to a pre-registration briefing session after application. There can be dropout at any point, although in the early stages of the process it is not always possible to be precise with respect to numbers, since initial telephone enquiries and invitations to attend an information session are not always recorded.

Less initial interest

Although there was a feeling among some local authorities that initial enquiries had not declined, without accurate monitoring it is difficult to be sure. One authority estimated a 50 per cent dropout between initial telephone call and attendance at the information session, but with no baseline data it is impossible to say whether the dropout level at this stage has changed.

Most key workers were of the opinion that fewer people were now achieving registration either due to dropout during the process or better vetting. Numbers attending information sessions are declining in many areas, and the dropout after these sessions can be very high. One example was provided where the percentage going on to make an application after attending an information session was 19 per cent for 1998 and 18 per cent for 1999. The main reason suggested for this dropout is that people become aware of what is involved, which does not match their initial expectations of the job. In a small survey conducted by one EYDCP, the most common reasons for not proceeding with application were finding another job and start-up costs.

Delays in registration

Delays in registration were also put forward as a reason for some dropout, for example police checks taking as long as five months in an Inner London authority and having to wait up to six months to attend pre-registration training in a Two-Tier authority. In this latter case, people did not make their application until after they had attended the training and received a home visit. Although most authorities said they met the statutory requirement of 12 weeks for registration, in reality there could be long delays before application. Furthermore, it was felt that applicants were more thoroughly vetted now and therefore more were not going on to register.

Whereas in the past, new registrations matched or outmatched the numbers of childminders cancelling their registration, more recently the trend has been for more cancellations combined with fewer new registrations. Thus in one county over a twelve-month period, there were 91 new registrations and 214 cancellations.

Reasons for fewer childminders

A similar picture emerged during our meetings with key workers in the NCMA and local authorities and the survey of EYDCPs. Time after time the same reasons were put forward for falling childminder numbers. These reasons tended to be based on ancecdotal information rather than empirical data. It appears that there is no one reason which can be said to account for the fall, but a combination of reasons. These reasons, described below, are contributing to a decrease in the supply of new childminders and an increase in the number who are leaving childminding.

Changing demographics and employment opportunities

More women are delaying childbirth and first establishing a career. When they do start a family they tend to have fewer children. They are therefore in a better position to return to work and pay for childcare. Consequently, the pool of women who do not have a career and are unable to afford childcare is shrinking. Childcare Tax Credit (CCTC) may also reduce the pool of women attracted to childminding, since help with childcare costs may make alternative employment more economical than was once the case. However, CCTC only came into effect in October 1999 and, if it is having an affect on the number of childminders, it is only very recent. At the same time, employment offering flexible working conditions has increased. This means that women with young children have more employment opportunities, usually offering better pay, less hassle and more opportunities to socialise. There has also been an expansion of employment opportunities within the childcare field, not only in other types of provision, but in the Childcare Information Service, EYDCPs, registration, inspection and development work. Women who gain experience and qualifications whilst childminding are often moving into other childcare-related work, which again offers greater financial reward.

Nature of the work

Childminding is low paid and has low status, which does not make it an attractive employment choice. Low status affects parents' demand for childminders because they believe group care offers better quality or a higher status. The DfEE's second survey of parental demand for childcare in 2001 will show whether parental demand for childminders has declined. The type of work that childminders are getting is changing too. There is a growing demand for part-time, sessional and non-traditional hours, reflecting the changes in working hours. The work is more piecemeal and, possibly as a consequence, less satisfying. Childminders have difficulty finding children to fill their 'slots' and make childminding financially

viable. Two of the ten former childminders in the case studies stopped childminding because they could not fill their vacancies. It was also considered by some that the restrictions on numbers and ages of children results in limitations to earning capacity.

The professionalisation of childminding had both positive and negative consequences on recruitment and retention, according to some key workers. There are now clear quality standards to be met and childminding is moving more towards a 'professional' service provided in the home. Yet training does not lead to increased status or the ability to charge more. Increased responsibility and greater awareness of their vulnerability to accusations of abuse was thought by some to be reason to leave and for others not to enter childminding. Additional paperwork and book-keeping also put some people off.

The NCMA officers and two local authorities suggested that the reason why some childminders were leaving was due to negative experiences with the Childcare Tax Credit. Childminders were being asked to sign forms and keep a place open, only to find that the child did not arrive and they lost income. One way volunteered to overcome this problem was to pay the credit directly to the childminder. Although, CCTC may be a reason why childminders are leaving their occupation now, its recent introduction means that CCTC cannot account for the steady decline in childminder numbers over the last three years.

Increase in other forms of provision

In Chapters One and Two we reported on the increase in places offered by other types of childcare provision, specifically day nurseries and out-of-school provision, and the extension of part-time education for three- and four-year olds. The fact that children, both the childminder's own and others, are starting school at an earlier age, may mean that a childminder stops childminding sooner than she once did. The increase in other types of provision was mentioned as a reason for falling childminder numbers at all our meetings with local authorities, and in many of the EYDCP returns where respondents had put forward their views.

For this project, we conducted an analysis of the figures published annually for day care facilities (DoH, 1997; DfEE, 2000). We looked at changes between 1997, 1998 and 1999. (Not all local authorities could be included, as some were split up during this period.) Changes in the numbers of childminders, day nurseries, playgroups and out-of-school services were correlated. If childminding were being replaced by other forms of day care, then areas with falls in the number of childminders should have had a corresponding rise in other forms of day care. This was not found. We found no relation between falling childminder numbers and a rise in any other form of provision. If anything, areas with a growth in other forms of care also had an increase in childminder numbers.

Regulation

There was the suggestion in some authorities, and from NCMA officers and development workers, that some people find the registration process too bureaucratic. Those who choose to childmind often did not have any formal qualifications and may find the process and expectations intimidating. People are generally now subjected to greater accountability in their jobs, but childminders who have been working in the home for many years sometimes have difficulty with this new

ethos. It has to be recognised that people start childminding for different reasons and while some approach it in professional terms, others may see it more in terms of a stop-gap. The latter may tend to be put off by the 'red tape' and hassle. As one interviewee pointed out, the administrative aspect of the job does not reduce in complexity whether it is someone looking after one child for a friend for a year and someone who is treating it as a professional job. In the case studies, four of the ten former childminders mentioned tighter regulations and bureaucracy as a reason for leaving.

Although the move to OFSTED was mentioned by everyone as a factor which may have an impact on recruitment and retention, many said that childminders' anxiety had been allayed by reassuring announcements that the changeover would not result in draconian inspection regimes.

Support

The first year of childminding is often a critical one, and where support may be most needed. Dropout can be high due to isolation, not getting work or as a result of a negative experience. Where demand is low, childminders find themselves taking children that perhaps they are too inexperienced to work with and the arrangement breaks down. For three of our case studies, who were former childminders, negative experiences with parents or children were the reasons given for stopping. Their experiences had resulted in either a lack of confidence or inability to cope with children/parents and the feeling that the job was not worth the aggravation.

The reducing levels and changing nature of childminder support, such as inspectors having less of a supportive role, was considered a

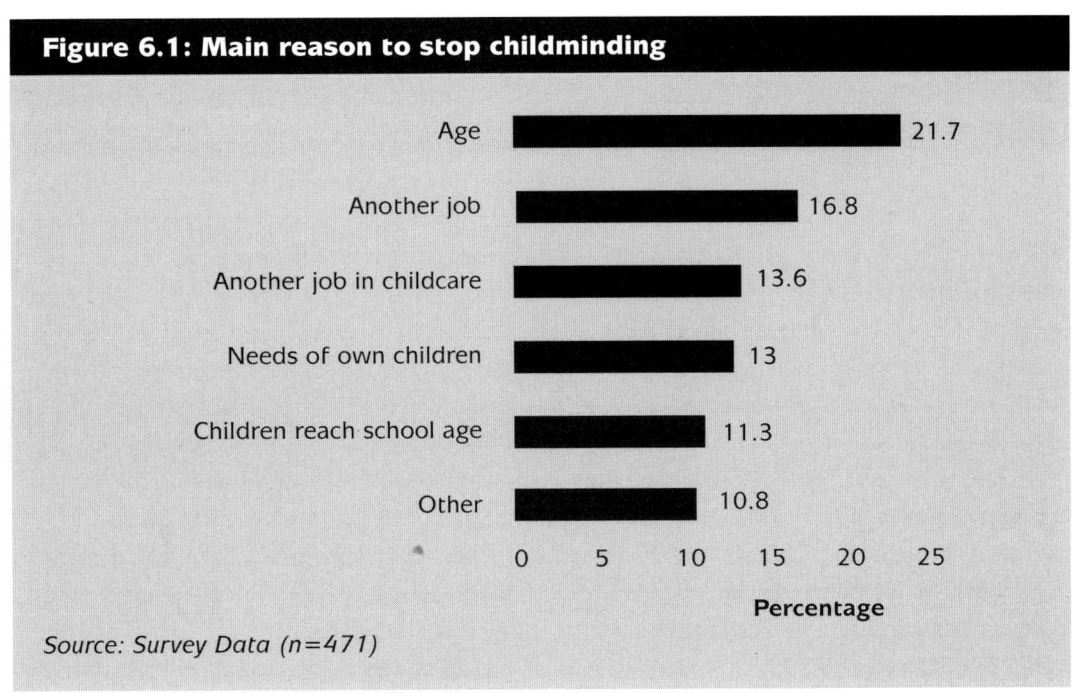

Figure 6.1: Main reason to stop childminding

Reason	Percentage
Age	21.7
Another job	16.8
Another job in childcare	13.6
Needs of own children	13
Children reach school age	11.3
Other	10.8

Source: Survey Data (n=471)

factor affecting retention. Many felt that more should be done to support childminders and the new childminder networks were seen as a positive step.

Reasons childminders give for leaving

There is very little empirical work on why childminders leave childminding. Exit interviews are conducted in a few authorities, usually a questionnaire to childminders who have cancelled their registration. Exit interviews, however, can have low response rates and people do not always give their reasons for leaving. Surveys have also been conducted as we report below, but information from these sources has limited value in helping us to understand the changes taking place, since we do not have baseline data with which to compare results.

In our survey of childminders, we asked all respondents what would be their main reason to stop childminding (Figure 6.1). Nearly a quarter gave their age as a reason for stopping, but almost a third (30 per cent) would stop because they had got another job, including another job in childcare. Moreover, if the reason that children reaching school-age were to be interpreted as the respondent now being able to work outside the home, the number of childminders surveyed who would stop because they wanted another job would rise to 42 per cent.

Of the 30 case studies, ten were former childminders. A number of reasons had influenced their decision to stop childminding and often it was a combination of reasons. These included:

- not being able to find work as a childminder (two);
- tighter regulations and frustrations with bureaucracy (four);
- negative experiences with parents or children (three);
- a feeling that it was time to move on (four),

particularly for those who had seen it as a stop-gap while their children were young, and;

- lack of career progression as a childminder (one).

Seven of the ten former childminders were working, although only two had remained in the childcare field, working as nannies. One former childminder was pursuing a course in computer studies and the remaining two were not working.

From the survey of EYDCPs, two Partnerships had conducted telephone surveys of childminders who had cancelled registration. In one Unitary Authority, 146 childminders who had cancelled registration over a 12-month period (1998/1999) were telephoned, with 89 successful contacts. The desire to do something else (30), the demands of their own family (24) and their own children reaching school age (16) were the most frequently mentioned reasons for stopping. In another authority, one survey attempted to contact 106 former childminders who had stopped childminding between July 1999 and February 2000. Of the 61 contacted, children now at school (12) and being able to have a job outside the home (16) were, if viewed together, the major reason for cancellation, followed by moving (20) and family circumstances (12). Worries about OFSTED taking over registration and inspection were not mentioned. Again, without baseline data it is impossible to know if there are any changes in the reasons childminders give for ceasing to childmind.

Summary

Over the last four years the numbers of childminders leaving childminding has not been matched by new registrations. The trend seems to be for fewer new registrations and, at the same time, a higher turnover rate. It would appear, though there is no comparable data, that there is a larger dropout during the registration process than in previous years, due to a number of factors including more thorough vetting, a mismatch between what is involved in the job and initial expectations, and delays in registration. Due to lack of records, it is difficult to say whether there is less expressed interest in childminding than in previous years.

There are several reasons suggested for cancelling registrations and for fewer new registrations. These include changing demographics, resulting in a shrinking supply of prospective childminders; increased employment opportunities offering flexible working patterns; childcare tax credit which may make alternative employment financially more attractive; low pay and poor status attached to the work; the changing nature of the work; increased regulatory demands and lack of support.

In a recent survey of childcare providers, childminders said that the major obstacles to childminding were the time it took to register with the local authority and to fill vacancies, and the lack of support for small businesses. The greatest obstacle to continuing as a childminder was financial viability (Callender, 2000). The increased number of places in other types of provision was also put forward by our respondents as a reason childminders are leaving, though an analysis at local government level did not provide evidence of this. This work on falling childminder numbers has shed light on what may be happening. A telephone survey of 250 former childminders, which is to be undertaken for the DfEE, will provide further information and add to our understanding of the situation.

7 | Conclusions and issues

Conclusions

We began this report with the main conclusions from a 1987 review of childminding research. This study shows strong continuities. Childminding continues to be mainly undertaken by women when they have younger children, as a means of enabling them to combine paid work and care for their own children. However, there is evidence to support the view that, while many childminders see childminding as a passing phase in their employment career, moving on to other work when their children are older, another substantial group do see childminding as a longer-term commitment.

Childminders generally still have low levels of education. Prior to having children, many have worked in less-skilled service-sector occupations. Pay and working conditions remain poor and insecure. Many childminders have vacancies, while the use parents make of childminders may be complex, often involving part-time arrangements; such flexibility may benefit parents, but not always childminders. There is a widespread feeling among childminders that their work is regarded by society as of low value. At the same time, they enjoy their work, expressing high levels of satisfaction.

New childminders face entry into a large childcare market. For many there are barriers to entry, both material (because of the costs of start-up, although these may now be eased by new government grants), and in terms of getting clients in competition with established providers. This is especially the case because many clients use informal and network methods of search in which importance attaches to word of mouth recommendations. Once established, there is a basic tension between being a carer, with its emphasis on commitment and affective engagement with children, and operating as a small business in a private childcare market, involving financial transactions with adults. The former may inhibit the latter. Other researchers have drawn attention to how parents (usually mothers) adopt a strategy of 'personalising the market', including building relationships with carers which emphasise the affective side of the relationship. This produces a 'necessary fiction', normally adhered to by both sides 'which obscures the naked financial exchange or striving for profit that underpins the childcare market' (Vincent and Ball, 1999). This suggests that many childminders are in a weak position as providers of care in the market.

Some of these issues arise from, or are at least exacerbated by, childminding being a form of home-work – and a unique form at that: for no other home-based occupation involves the home worker caring for others. Home working brings advantages for childminders. But it also involves complex relationships with parents and regulatory authorities, which can generate particular tensions and difficulties. For example, there are boundaries to be determined and maintained: between being a worker, mother and wife; between your own and minded children; between home, family and clients. Or, to take another example, inspection, whether by parents or regulators, involves intrusion into private space, a feeling of 'completely strange people in your house'.

Childminding and mothering are closely linked. At a practical level, most childminders are mothers themselves and care for their own children; at the conceptual level, the work is often understood in terms of substitute mothering (and providing a home-like environment). Childminders want to be viewed as professional childcare workers, yet the need for training and qualification is less strongly felt, with some seeing personal experience of motherhood as the most important requirement. There remains some ambivalence, among some parents as well as some childminders, as to whether childminding is an occupation – and if so, what kind of occupation it is.

Despite these problems, childminding continues to play an important role in the provision of childcare. Childminders remain, for the moment at least, the most widespread providers of formal care. Childminders and nurseries have a similar user profile, providing mainly for full-time working parents and for parents in high-status jobs, the main growth area in parental employment.

There are, however, clear signs that the numbers working in this occupation are declining. Several factors appear to lie behind this recent fall in numbers, including alternative employment opportunities. It remains to be seen whether government policies and increasing demand for childcare will reverse the decline.

Issues

There can be no doubt that childminding is a major occupation in the childcare field. Childminders provide an important paid service to working parents and their children. Issues are raised about the future of the occupation, notably:

- the identity of the occupation – who is the childminder?
- the standing of the occupation – how is childminding valued?
- recruitment and retention – what is the future for childminding?

At present, there are limited understandings of early childhood work, across the childcare and early years field. Two main concepts can currently be discerned: the worker as substitute mother ('child carer') (Singer, 1993) and the worker as school teacher. Neither, however, is an appropriate or useful concept for the future of childminding – nor indeed for the future of early childhood work in general.

The current understanding of school teacher involves a narrow educational role confined to work with children over the age of three years, very different to the more holistic approach to children and their needs – both under and over three – demanded of a childminder. The concept of substitute mother applied to childminders is problematic for other reasons. It confounds fundamentally different relationships and roles; it belies the increasing expectations placed on childminders in relation to learning and providing services for 'children in need'; and it is based on a misconception that any woman (or at least any mother) is naturally capable of working with children.

Other possible understandings of early years work have been discussed in relation to centre-based provision, for example the 'early years teacher' and the 'pedagogue'. Both encompass work with children under and over three and a holistic approach to children (Moss, 2000). But are these any more appropriate for childminding? Are there other more appropriate concepts? What is needed, we would argue, is a rethinking of all work with young children, leading to a reconceptualisation which can incorporate the full range of current occupations, including teachers, workers in nurseries and other centres – and childminders. We shall return to this point.

Rethinking work with young children raises questions about its value. Can the pervasive poverty of childminders' training, pay and status be eradicated? The new tax credit may lead to improved pay, and new opportunities for training and working as members of networks are emerging. It remains to be seen, however, what impact these initiatives will have on the generality of childminders, even if take-up of the tax credit were to increase (recent reports estimate that four out of five single-parent families eligible for the benefit are not receiving help (Nursery World, 2000)). Another possibility would be the development of salaried childminders, with pay and conditions linked to training. But this option requires two conditions, both uncertain in Britain: that childminders are willing to cede their independence to assume employee status; and that public policy shifts from subsidising some parents (through tax credits) to subsidising all providers (through the payment of salaries). Moreover, neither option guarantees a substantial improvement in training, pay and status, depending as they do on what level of training and pay government is prepared to subsidise.

A central issue is whether childminding can be rethought and revalued in isolation, apart from other types of work with young children, or more generally apart from the wider context of 'care work'. Care work includes all forms of 'child care', as well as 'social care' which spans a wide range of services in the welfare sector (for example, for the growing numbers of very elderly people). For there are striking similarities between these occupational areas, which suggest shared and deep-seated causes of devaluation.

Care work, whether with children or adults, whether labelled 'child care' or 'social care', and whether centre-based or home-based, is highly gendered: care work, in its various forms, remains women's work. It is characterised by poor training, poor pay and other conditions, and low status. Gender and poor work are linked through a rationale that understands care work as something essentially female, at which women are naturally competent, needing little or no aptitude or training.

But there are changes occurring that may force rethinking and revaluation, if a crisis in care work is to be avoided. Britain, like many other wealthy countries, is facing an increasing demand for care work, not only in the child care area, as parental employment increases, but also in social care, as the population ages. Until now, the supply of labour for care work has depended heavily on a particular group – women with low levels of education, low levels of relevant training or none at all, and prepared (or needing) to work for low wages.

The treatment of care workers might be considered unacceptable, for its devaluation of important work and its exploitation of those doing this work. But it may also be unsustainable in a situation where the demand for care work of all kinds is increasing and the supply of labour is reducing, as the pool of women with low levels of education contracts and as alternative employment opportunities increase. The 1999/2000 report of the Chief Inspector of Social Services (2000), for example, points to acute staffing problems in the social care field, adding that 'many posts in social care offer less pay than less demanding jobs in supermarkets' (page 7).

The declining numbers of childminders, combined with other evidence such as the recruitment and retention problems in the social care workforce, should be taken as a warning sign: current assumptions about, and conditions in, care work may be unsustainable in the long term. This might lead to (at least) two responses. The first involves seeking new supplies of cheap labour, for example from welfare recipients or by immigration (see the discussion by Hochschild (2000) of the increasing influx of women from poor countries to the United States, to provide child care and other services). This seems to us problematic, not least because it fails to address deep-seated issues about the nature of the work and its value.

The second response involves taking a broad and strategic view of care work, both child care and social care, as well as related fields such as teaching. This requires bringing together government departments, notably the Department of Health and the Department for Education and Employment, and other interested organisations to do some 'joined up' thinking across these fields. The starting point needs to be the reconceptualisation of work with children and adults, producing new understandings which can accommodate *inter alia* a holistic approach to children and adults, the close relationship between caring and learning, and new thinking about the meanings of caring, learning and knowledge in a post-industrial, knowledge society. This process will also address the similarities and differences involved in working with different age groups, for example younger and older children, young people and elderly people.

These new understandings can then inform a range of decisions: about occupational structures (what types of workers are needed for which groups?), about training (what type and level of training do these workers require?) and about pay (what is the value of the work?). In our view, rethinking and revaluing the occupation of childminding should properly take place in this wider context.

References

Atkinson, A.M. (1991). 'Providers' evaluations of family day care services'. *Early Child Development and Care*, 68, 113–123.

Brannen, J., Moss, P., Owen, C. and Wale, C. (1997). *Mothers, fathers and employment*. DfEE Research Report 10.

Bridgewood, A. and Savage, P. (1993). *General Household Survey 1991*. London: HMSO.

Bull, J., Cameron, C., Candappa, M., Moss, P. and Statham, J. (1994). *Implementing the Children Act*. London: HMSO.

Callender, C. (2000). *The barriers to childcare provision*. DfEE Research Report RR231. London: DfEE.

Cameron, C., Owen, C., Moss, P (forthcoming). *Entry, Retention and Loss: a study of childcare students and workers*. (DfEE Research Report). London: DfEE

Candappa, M., Bull, J. Cameron, C., Moss, P. and Owen, C. (1996). *Policy into Practice: day care services for children under eight*. London: The Stationery Office.

Chief Inspector of Social Services (2000). *Modern social services, a commitment to people: the 9th Annual Report of the Chief Inspector of Social Services*. London: Department of Health.

Clyde, M. and Rodd, J. (1994). 'More than Just Baby-sitters: Family Day Care Providers' Perceptions of the Caregiving Role'. *Australian Journal of Early Childhood*, 19 (2) 37–42.

Daniel, W.W. (1980). *Maternity rights: the experience of women*. London: Policy Studies Institute.

Department for Education and Employment (1998). *Meeting the childcare challenge: a framework and consultation document* (Cm.3959). London: DfEE

Department for Education and Employment (1999a). *Statistics of education. Children's day care facilities at 31 March 1999, England*. London: The Stationery Office.

Department for Education and Employment (1999b). GCSE/GNVQ and GCEA/AS/Advance GNVQ result, for young people in England, 1998/99 (Provisional). SFR 35/1999.

Department for Education and Employment (2000). *Statistics of education: children's day care facilities at 31 March 2000, England*. DfEE Bulletin 08/00.

Department of Health (1991). *The Children Act 1989 Guidance and Regulations: Volume 2. Family support, day care and educational provision for young children*. London: HMSO

Department of Health (1997). *Children's day care facilities at 31 March 1996, England* (AF96/6). London: DoH.

Dillon, J. and Statham, J. (1998a). 'Placed and paid for: a national overview of the use of private and voluntary day care facilities for children in need'. *Child and Family Social Work*, 3, 113–123.

Dillon, J. and Statham, J. (1998b). *Sponsored day care for children in need: examples from twelve local authorities*. Report available from Thomas Coram Research Unit, Institute of Education, University of London

Employers' Organisation/Improvement and Development Agency (1999). *Registered childminders workforce survey 1998*. London: EO/IDeA.

Felstead, A. and Jewson, N. (1996). *Homeworkers in Britain*. London: HMSO.

Felstead, A. and Jewson, N. (2000). *In work at home: towards an understanding of homeworking*. London: Routledge.

Ferri, E., (1992). *What makes childminding work*. London: National Children's Bureau

Fischer, J.L and Eheart, B.K. (1991). 'Family day care: A theoretical basis for improving quality'. *Early Childhood Research Quarterly*, 6, 549–563.

Fosburg, S. (1981). *Family day care in the United States: summary of findings. Final report of the National Day Care Home Study*. Washington, DC: US Department of Health and Human Services.

Gelder, U. (1998). *Childminding: does it work for women?* Paper presented at the Social Policy Association Annual Conference, July 1998.

Hochschild, A. (2000). In Giddens, A. and Hutton, W. (eds.) *On the edge*. London: Vintage

Holtermann, S., Brannen, J., Moss, P. and Owen, C. (1999). *Lone parents and the labour market: Results from the 1997 Labour Force Survey and Review of Research* (ESR23), Sheffield: Employment Service

Howes, C. (1983). 'Caregiver behaviour in centre and family day care'. *Journal of Applied Developmental Psychology*, 4, 99–107.

Huws, U. (1994). *Key results from the national survey of homeworkers*. Leeds: National Group of Homeworking.

Karlsson, M. (1995). *Family day care in Europe*. Report for the EC Childcare Network. Brussels: European Commission Equal Opportunities Unit

Kids Clubs Network, 2000, 'The childcare revolution: facts and figures for 1999'. London: Kids Clubs Network.

Kontos, S., Howes, C., Shinn, M. and Galinsky, E. (1995). *Quality in family child care and relative care*. New York, NY: Teachers College Press, Columbia University.

La Valle, I., Finch S., Nove, A., Lewin, C. (2000). *Parents' Demand for Childcare*. London:DfEE.

Marsh, A. and McKay, S. (1993). 'Families, work and the use of child care', *Employment Gazette* August 361–370.

Martin, J. and Roberts, C. (1984). *Women and Employment: a lifetime perspective*. London: HMSO

Martin, S. and Plewis, I. (1991). Stability in day care arrangements. Paper presented at the British Psychological Society, London Conference, December 1991.

Mayall, B. and Petrie, P. (1983). *Childminding and day nurseries: what kind of care?* London: Heinemann.

McRae, S. and Daniel, D. (1991). *Maternity rights in Britain: the experience of women and employers*. London: Policy Studies Institute

Meltzer, H. (1994). *Day care services for children*. London: HMSO.

Molgaard, V.K. (1993). 'Caregivers' perceptions of the relationship between the family day care business and their own families', *Child and Youth Care Forum*, 22 (1) 55–71.

Mooney A. and Munton, A.G. (1999). 'The role of self-assessment in the regulation and inspection of group day care', *Children and Society*, 13, 94–105.

Mooney, A. and Munton, A.G. (1998). Quality in early childhood services: parent, provider and policy perspectives. *Children and Society*, 12, 101–112.

Mooney, A. and Munton, A.G. (1997). *Research and policy in early childhood services: time for a new agenda*. London: Institute of Education

Moss, P., Owen, C., Statham, J., Bull, J., Cameron, C. and Candappa, M. (1995). *Survey of day care providers in England and Wales: a Working Paper from the TCRU Children Act Project*. London: Thomas Coram Research Unit, Institute of Education, University of London

Moss, P. (2000). 'Training of early childhood education and care staff', *International Journal of Educational Research*, 33, 31–53

Moss, P., Dillon, J. and Statham, J. (2000). 'The 'child in need' and 'the rich child': discourses, constructions and practice', *Critical Social Policy*, 20(2), 233–254

Moss, P. (1987). *Review of childminding research* (Thomas Coram Research Unit Occasional Paper No.5). London: Thomas Coram Research Unit, Institute of Education, University of London

Nelson, M.K. (1989). 'Negotiating care: relationships between family daycare providers and mothers', *Feminist Studies*, 15 (1) 7–33.

Nelson, M.K. (1994). 'Family day care providers: dilemmas of daily practice' in Nakano, E. (Eds.) *Mothering: ideology, experience, agency*. New York, NY: Routledge.

Nursery World, 2000, 'Low take-up of tax credit by lone parents sparks debate', 12 October

Pence, A.R. and Goelman, H. (1991). 'The relationship of regulation, training, and motivation to quality of care in family day care', *Child and Youth Care Forum*, 20 (2), 83–101.

Phizacklea, A. and Wolkowitz, C. (1995). *Homeworking women*. London: Sage.

Rose, M. (1999) *Explaining and forecasting job satisfaction: the contribution of occupational profiling*. Bath, University of Bath.

Saggers, S., Grant, J., Woodhead, M. and Banham, V. (1994). 'The professionalisation of mothering: family day care', *The Australian and New Zealand Journal of Sociology*. 30 (3) 273–287.

Singer, E. (1993). 'Shared care for children', *Theory and Psychology*, 3(4) 429–49.

Statham, J., Dillon, J. and Moss, P. (2000). 'Sponsored day care in a changing world', *Children and Society*, 14, 23–36

Taylor, A.R., Dunster, L. and Pollard, J. (1999). 'And this helps me how?: family child care providers discuss training', *Early Childhood Research Quarterly*, 14 (3) 285–312.

Thair, T. and Risden, A. (1999). 'Women in the labour market: results from the spring 1998 LFS', *Labour Market Trends*, 107(3) 85–152.

Thomson, K. (1996). 'Working mothers: choice or circumstance?' In R. Jowell, J. Curtice, A. Park, L. Brook, D. Ahrendt and K. Thomson (eds.) *British Social Attitudes: The 12th Report*. Aldershot: Dartmouth.

Vincent, C. and Ball, S.J. (1999). 'A market in love? Choosing pre-school child care'. Paper presented for the British Educational Research Association Conference, Sussex, September, 1999.

Whitebook, M., Howes, C. and Phillips, D. (1989). *Who cares? child care yeachers and the uality of care in America*. Final report of the National Child Care Staffing Study. Oakland, CA: Child Care Employee Project.